I CAN'T
GET OVER
MY PARTNER'S
AFFAIR

I CAN'T GET OVER MY PARTNER'S AFFAIR

50 QUESTIONS about recovering from extreme betrayal and the long-term impact of infidelity

ANDREW G. MARSHALL

MARSHALL METHOD
PUBLISHING

The letters in this book are from people who have written to me via my website and the case histories are based on persons with whom I have worked in my therapy practice. Their details have been changed to protect confidentiality.

Marshall Publishing Method
London • Florida
www.marshallmethodpublishing.com

ISBN: 978-0-9929718-8-5

A CIP catalogue record for this book is available from the British Library

Cover and interior design: Gary A. Rosenberg • www.thebookcouple.com

Printed in the UK by TJ International, Padstow, Cornwall

CONTENTS

To Alice who didn't give up,
learnt a lot in the process
and shared her journey with me.

INTRODUCTION

You want to forgive and move on from your partner's infidelity. Your children would be heartbroken if you split up but recovery seems an impossible mountain to climb. Your partner is full of remorse and says he or she wants to save your relationship but often you doubt it. Perhaps he or she is still in contact with the affair partner or moody and difficult – which is doubly painful after what he or she's put you through – or becomes evasive or angry if you try to pin down what exactly has happened. No wonder you swing between thinking it will be OK and fearing that if you STILL can't get over the affair that your marriage must be doomed. Don't worry, you're not alone!

One in seven divorces are granted on the grounds of infidelity in the UK (according to the Office for National Statistics) but this is just the tip of the iceberg. Research commissioned by Grant Thornton – the financial and business advice group – of one hundred leading matrimonial lawyers found an affair was the primary cause of marriage breakdown in 32 per cent of couples seeking their help. This figure is up 10 per cent since 2005. Over a similar period, the number of people hiring private investigators – to find out just what their partner has been up to – has risen from just 18 per cent to a staggering 49 per cent. Meanwhile a separate study for the Internet Research Institute of Oxford University found similar levels of distrust with 44 per cent of spouses checking their partner's phones and reading their private texts and emails. In the US, the number of women admitting to having an affair has risen by 40 per cent over the past two decades and has reached 14.7 per cent of all wives. The number of men committing adultery at some point in their marriage has held constant at 21 per cent of all husbands (according to the National Opinion Research Center's Social Survey).

Since writing the international bestseller *How Can I Ever Trust You Again?*, I've had hundreds of letters from people who were struggling to truly forgive and find a future together. I've also counselled countless couples who have seen other therapists but were still stuck. So what's kept all these people bogged down in the aftermath of an affair despite all the excellent books, helpful advice on the Internet and skilled counsellors? I think there are three problems.

Firstly, there is an unhelpful myth – which I hear time and time again when I appear on the TV, radio or am interviewed for newspapers – that affairs are resolved pretty quickly. You discover your partner has been cheating and either throw him or her out or after lots of tears decide to forgive and forget. If I asked the TV hosts and journalists to speculate on how long this process would take they'd probably say a month – three months at tops. I wish it was this simple because I know from 30 years working with couples that the pain is overwhelming, we hate uncertainty and long to believe the myth that infidelity can be sorted out quickly – once and for all. When I wrote my book, I stressed over and over again that the first year is the worst and how easy it is to get stuck into the recovery process. However, I didn't want to push the message too hard because it's really depressing if you've just discovered infidelity – and that's the majority of the buyers of these books. I can be more straightforward here because you know from first-hand experience how recovery can often seem two steps forward and three back. To be honest, I don't consider it particularly unusual or worrying if couples are still struggling with the aftermath of an affair two years after recovery. I've also seen people dealing with the fall-out five years later and STILL been able to help them move on together. I hope that is more reassuring than scary.

Secondly, in the last five years, affairs have become increasingly toxic and recovery more complex. There are hook-up sites and apps designed to facilitate 'easy' sex, and while previously it was unusual for someone to be cheating with multiple partners, I'm afraid that it's become only too common. The more widespread acceptance of pornography – which markets itself as another branch of the entertainment industry – facilitates access to professional sex partners. On most porn sites users are just one click away from a prostitute. The increased competition between pornographers has made their material more explicit and more likely to feature kinky stuff and 'special interests'. So in the aftermath of an affair, when most people do a forensic search of their partner's web history, they are uncovering not only tastes their partner has kept secret but those which actually disgusts them.

Even if the infidelity had been relatively normal and understandable – drinks were involved, a line was crossed and it only happened a couple of times – it is much harder to put the past behind you. Facebook, Twitter and other social media provide a never-ending stream of updates about the affair partner. Mobile phones allow someone to ping a message into your home at any time of the day or night – while in the past, affair partners who were up late night drinking and getting maudlin would have had to get in their car, risk arrest for drunk drinking and come round to ring your front door bell. The same technology also allows the discoverer of the affair to read all the messages between the affair partners, which means that particularly hurtful phrases get stuck in their minds. If they are particularly unlucky, like some of my clients, they will discover short films or pictures of their partner having sex with another woman or man.

Our culture has shifted in other ways that make it harder to recover from infidelity. Men and women are more likely to be friends – something that was much rarer 30 years ago when I started out as a marital therapist. So I have many clients where the unfaithful partner thinks its OK to remain 'friends' with their affair partner and accuse their partner of being 'controlling' if he or she is uncomfortable with the idea. Worse still, while new technology has made it easier than ever before to stray, our society is becoming more judgmental – not only of the 'cheaters' but the men and women who try to 'stand by' them. So my clients report that their friends are sometimes critical of their decision to work on their marriage and claim 'I would have more self-respect'. Even if friends are supportive in the first few months, they lose patience when it drags on and on. With everyone so down on infidelity – even though it is more common – it also feels as though you are being 'disloyal' to your partner if you reveal the full extent of his or her behaviour. The result is that the discoverer, who needs lots of support and tender loving care (TLC), is left feeling either alone or exposed.

The third problem is that when couples get stuck, they imagine something must be fundamentally wrong with their relationship. However, in most cases, the problem is the depth of the pain of the betrayal. This means people need more time to recover (and shouldn't beat themselves up for not making faster progress) and could need more specialist support and different coping strategies (than those designed for couples at the beginning of the discovery process).

How to use this book

I wrote this book to explain about the problems of extreme betrayal: by which I mean multiple partners, cheating with your best friend, a long-term affair, unsavoury sexual discoveries, being childhood sweethearts (and therefore have had no other sexual partners) or had such a close relationship that infidelity seems a double slap. It also includes people who yo-yo back and forth between their lover and their partner and end up shredding everybody's nerves – including their own. In addition, I wanted to discuss the long-term impact of infidelity, so you don't feel like the only couple in the world still wading through the aftermath of discovery.

I have 50 letters and 50 answers to frequently asked questions about infidelity. They are arranged into groups but please read them all – even if they don't immediately apply – because it is reassuring to discover that others' circumstances might be worse, and sometimes an extreme example can better illustrate a wider point. With each letter, I've also highlighted a key reason why each correspondent might be stuck. At the end of the book, I've gathered up all the advice and drawn on clients in counselling to provide a strategy to help you break through your deadlock and find a way forward.

If you and your partner are trying to save your marriage but your conversations drop into a well-worn loop (which is both painful and unproductive), you might read the book together. I've had clients who have taken *What is Love?* – which also features readers' questions – and taken it in turns to read out one of the letters, for each person to then give their advice and finally read out my reply. They found other people's dilemmas threw new light on their own and helped them discuss contentious issues without everything becoming too personal.

Finally, I want to give a bit of reassurance for times when everything seems bleak. It is a real asset that you are still hanging in there fighting for your marriage. I am full of admiration for my clients who are determined to root out all the problems in the marriage, rather than settle down into a false peace or give up and move on without truly exploring what went wrong, and who keep striving to truly get over their partner's affair.

Andrew G. Marshall
www.andrewgmarshall.com

THE QUESTIONS

WHAT IF I CAN'T GET MY HEAD ROUND MY PARTNER'S AFFAIR?

1. I am 26 years old, I work with my partner and used to work with the girl he had an affair with. She bullied me, encouraged him to cancel our wedding plans just ten weeks before the day, claimed to him and many others that I was mentally unstable, and made him stay out all night so that I would leave him. The last thing she did was the worst – she deprived him of the right to tell me of any misgivings himself – she did it in the middle of the working day in our office.

We separated in February and were apart until June. Our separation was a consequence of his affair, though he believed I was none the wiser at the time, as I had not challenged him about it for fear of making a false accusation about something so serious. She waited until she discovered that we were back together again to tell me. I had just agreed to move back in with him when she did it; I had just spent £1,000 on terminating the contract on my tenancy, so I was forced to move in with him due to the financial and contractual obligations I was facing. I got back together with him although I was certain they'd been together, but until she told me I had always hoped that there was no 'overlap' in the relationships. That was three months ago.

She's no longer around, and while I am pleased about not

seeing her every day, I feel deprived of the right to discuss the matter with her – she bullied me for months and spread lies and rumours to appease her own guilt (she was also violent towards me on one occasion). I would like just five minutes to tell her that there's more to life than placing your guilt and pain on others, and that I genuinely hope she finds her inner peace one day. That said, she's the least of my worries.

Despite what my partner did, he remains the most loyal and well-respected person in my life. I am angry, hurt and disappointed by his actions and I feel a deep sense of loss in my faith in mankind, but I love him so much that I ache, and I would give anything and everything to remove enough of the pain so I may enjoy our future together without the burden of the past ten months.

The problem is, I feel just terrible right now. I've lived in shock for weeks, have spent the past three months on sleeping medication and am on high alert with mental health teams. I have avoided telling family and friends of the ordeal in case they express their negative feelings too liberally – I have enough of my own and cannot manage theirs as well.

I have spent so much of the past few weeks hating him, avoiding his affection, and wishing someone would remove me from this mess and offer enough financial relief that I might start again elsewhere. I somehow know that these thoughts are emotionally driven by grief, and with time they should pass and make way for a happy future, but how do I know this for sure? He is desperate to try and rebuild my trust, but all I can do at the moment is punish him. How long can I expect it to take before I can relax a bit more and start to feel like our relationship really can benefit from this experience? I believe that it is possible, but working through it emotionally is another matter entirely.

Andrew writes:

What a horrible experience. I'm not surprised that you're finding it hard to recover. Financial problems, infidelity and bullying! So I want to offer some reassurance, you're doing really well – in fact better than I would expect just three months into discovering such systematic lies and betrayal.

It's perfectly normal to feel shocked – it's nature's way of cushioning the impact. Just accept that's where you need to be, at the moment, because adding a layer of self-criticism for being on high alert will just deepen your distress. Over the coming months, you will begin to go through seven stages on your journey from discovery to recovery. In fact, you've already begun to cross over from the first stage – *Shock and Disbelief* – into the second one: *Intense Questioning*. You could even have started to engage with the issues of stage three: *Decision Time* – where you start to digest everything you've discovered about his infidelity and engage with whether it's possible or even wise to continue in this relationship. I know you want to feel normal again, but trying to rush ahead will add to your stress.

So let's try and break down the issues into manageable chunks. As you say, the Other Woman (OW) is reasonably straightforward. Instead of thinking about speaking to her for five minutes, write a long angry letter telling her about your feelings towards her and how you've risen above her stupid little games. Although it will help get the pain out of your system, please don't send the letter. (Otherwise, you'll have another round of her interfering in your life.)

As for your relationship with your boyfriend, it sounds like you're angry with him too but because you've been so keen to remove the burden of the last ten months, you've eaten all that anger and it is sitting in a cold hard undigested lump in your stomach. Therefore, I think that you really should talk to your friends and family. Yes, they will be angry but that's not a bad thing as it will probably bring some of your anger up to the surface. Even better, they will be able to support you and you'll stop feeling so alone with this pain.

After *Decision Time*, comes stage four of recovery after infidelity and I call this one: *Hope*. It comes as a huge relief after months of unhappiness and uncertainty. You begin to believe that your relationship can not only recover but emerge stronger and better from the experience.

You ask how long this nightmare is going to carry on for... I'm afraid people can be trapped in stage five – *Attempted Normality* – for years. This is where it seems everything is back to normal but the partner who discovered the affair still has to deal with the aftershocks. Meanwhile, the partner who has been unfaithful is full of guilt and shame. Looking at your situation, you still need to start to learn the lessons from the affair – like why did he cheat and keep on lying even when trying to rebuild your marriage? Why couldn't he talk about his cold feet over your marriage and instead ran into the arms of this OW? Why do you put up with being bullied and find it hard to stand up for yourself? This process is really tough, so I call the sixth stage: *Despair – Bodies Float to the Surface*. The bodies are the issues that you knew were there but chose not to exhume or sometimes were not even aware of. Once they have been properly examined, you can reach the final destination and seventh stage: *Intense Learning*.

Assuming that you begin to get to the bottom of this situation – and let the bodies float up to the surface – I normally find that people feel significantly better 12 months after the final revelation of infidelity. I know that sounds a long way off but be brave and don't expect too much from yourself too soon.

Why can't I get over his affair? *It is early days in the recovery process.*

2.

Four months ago I discovered my husband had been having a two-year affair with a work colleague (who was also a very good friend to me). I find it hard to put into words the feelings and devastation I felt and still feel. It physically hurts so much especially because during the affair period we were in the process of adopting a child. The OW was a very close friend and work colleague and knew things about our relationship which others didn't (when we had a row, when things were tough, etc) our children and hers were also close and when we finally adopted our daughter she even joined us on our first family holiday.

My husband had a new job, and we moved away, but after I discovered the affair he said this was because he wanted to end it so much that he felt it was the only way to protect us. Since the discovery, he has cut all contact with her and we have read and used resources on the Internet to help us. He says he loves me and wants me more than anything. He made a stupid, stupid mistake which then snowballed and he couldn't manage it and was so scared that she would reveal what had happened if he finished it.

We have worked hard and talked and listened to each other, but I struggle so much with images and thoughts in my head of them together being intimate with one another. I know I want to make our marriage and relationship work; he is my best friend and I want to be with him. I just want to make these things go away. We are working together through your book *How Can I Ever Trust You Again?* and are finding it very useful. However, I struggle with images of my husband being unfaithful and want to know how to deal with them. Thank you for your time.

Andrew writes:

First, I want to congratulate you on working so hard and listening, and to your husband for making such a clean break. I can't tell you how much of a difference than makes. Next, I want to reassure you that four months is early days in recovering from an affair (especially as it went on for a relatively long time and you knew the OW so well).

So what to do about the images and thoughts? If they keep coming back, I think we should take them seriously (and they could also be telling us something important). However, I think it is important to separate the images from the thoughts – especially as I suspect they are coming from different places, ie the images from your unconscious and the thoughts from the front of your mind.

If the images are coming when you're awake, don't push them away or get angry with yourself or worry 'I'll never get over them'. Allow yourself to watch if it is like a clip of film, or if it appears as a still image, to examine the photo. When you have finished, write a summary of the film or what the picture is about. I would also like you to add your feelings – but with no thoughts attached. Please accept the feelings and witness them (rather than judging yourself for having them). They are a natural response to something traumatic. Afterwards, do something soothing – have a bath, cup of tea or phone a friend. When you have a body of evidence, ask yourself, What are these images telling me? What are the themes? What can I learn from them?

If the images are part of a dream, it's basically the same process. Be conscious that you're dreaming, don't fight it, and when you wake up, lie still as this helps you to remember. Keep a pen and paper by the bed and jot down a few keys words as this will also help to tie down the details. Once again, ask yourself: What is my subconscious trying to tell me? (By the way, don't worry – dreams are not predictors of what's going to happen.)

When you have the images – or the affair is particularly troubling

– consider telling your husband. He probably knows – because you've become distant or angry – and this gives him permission to talk. You could even tell him the basic details. However, and this is key, he does not have to do anything about the image (this feeling of powerlessness to make it better is what makes men angry or ashamed about their past behaviour and end up pushing their wives away). Your husband just needs to listen, give you a hug and say something reassuring like 'We will get through this'.

Moving on to the thoughts, once again rather than trying to push them away or edit them, write them down – almost like you're taking dictation. When you've finished, we move on to a separate and different approach. While I want you to accept your feelings, I want you to also challenge your thoughts. Now they are out of your head and on paper, cross out anything that seems ludicrous. Look for words like, 'never' and 'always' – what is the evidence that you will 'never get over it'. Change these thoughts to something more appropriate: 'It will take a long time to get over it.' OK, it's a small change but a significant one and – THIS IS IMPORTANT – thoughts influence feelings. If you think 'never', the feelings will be panic, anxiety or even despair. If you think 'a long time' it could be 'annoyance' (for him putting you in this place) or 'determined' (to push onwards).

When analysing your thoughts, it helps to change statements into questions. For example, 'I can't get over this' becomes 'How can I get over this?' By this point, you should be feeling calmer, as you've been able to cross out some statements, watered down others and moved into problem-solving mode.

More times than not, there is something that has promoted this over-thinking or brought images up to the surface. I call it the animating spark, which is normally something quite small – for example, it's your birthday and you're wondering why he didn't come home early last year on this date. If this is the case, address the animating spark calmly with your husband. You'll find it is much easier to resolve a specific question than a torrent of problems, thoughts and fears all tumbling out at once.

Why can't I get over my husband's affair? *Recovery is not a straight line.*

3. If my wife is having an affair with another married man, who has children and they are conspiring an elaborate way to get out of his marriage and our marriage, leaving a wake of destruction behind, my question is:

Should I tell HIS wife that he is having an affair with MY wife and that his plans are to leave her broken with nothing and two children to look after?

If I do tell his wife, should I do it anonymously or not? He will not tell his wife until he has conspired to get all his ducks in a row that suits him best and not her.

Andrew writes:

You are in a highly charged situation and the stakes are very high. So it's good that you've stepped back and begun to think everything through.

I'm going to start by answering your question (because I doubt you'll focus on the second part of what I have to say until I do), but I'd like you to ask yourself some questions (which I think will be of far greater use in the long run).

So should you tell your spouse's affair partner's other half? This tactic is fraught with danger and there are two particularly dangerous outcomes. Firstly, you stop the affair but your wife never forgives you (because you have gone behind her back, ruined the marriage of someone she loves or proved that you are a 'complete bastard' who disregards her wishes). I know you can argue – and I agree – she's gone behind your back, he brought it on himself and what else could you do. However, what counts is what she thinks! Anyway, you want her to *choose* to end the affair rather than be forced (and end up having secret Facebook chats, etc). In this way, you win a battle but lose the war. Secondly, you could force everything out into the open but her affair partner leaves his wife and he's now more available/appealing (and more likely to undermine attempts to save your marriage) or they simply run away together tomorrow.

There are other alternatives. You could just threaten your wife that you will tell his wife. However, I don't think you can threaten someone into loving you! You could speak to the other man and tell him that if doesn't back off, you'll tell his wife. There is a possibility that he might realise what he has to lose, but coming across like an angry parent (telling him what's best for his marriage and generally attacking him) is just as likely to make him start behaving like a rebellious teenager (and putting two fingers up to you both literally and metaphorically). Remember, every word that you say will be reported back to your wife – with the worst possible spin.

In all these options, you have given your wife more ammunition to say you're the problem. Worse still, he becomes the victim of your attack and she has to ride to his rescue (and you've bonded them together even stronger, so it's poor little star-crossed lovers versus the rest of the world). Although you're justifying your behaviour on his wife's 'right to know', I doubt you'd get much thanks from her either. My guess is she probably does know deep down and is, for reasons of her own, putting her fingers in her ears and going la la la. There's no point trying to do this anonymously either, as they will KNOW it's you and you'll get the rap plus an extra dose of scorn and hatred for 'not having the courage to come out and say it' or 'sneaking around'. (Again, I know this is the pot calling the kettle black, but do you want to be right or married?)

15

So what should you do? I want you to step back and look at your thoughts and beliefs. In all your going over and over stuff in your mind, you have taken small snippets of information, put your interpretation on them and converted that into a solid fact. Let me give you an example, 'He is planning to leave her broke with two children to care for'. What is the evidence? How could you possibly know his motives? (I doubt you even know your own motives or feelings, which probably keep changing from revenge to forgiveness, and back again.) Are you truly an independent witness? How do you know they are waiting to 'line their ducks up'? What are these ducks? Could they equally be frightened, indecisive and vacillating? Perhaps he does love his children and doesn't want to break up his family but can't give up his affair? Perhaps he's just an ordinary guy caught between a rock and a hard place rather than how you paint him: A Bond villain on a secret island stroking his cat.

Instead of focusing on this other man – who is probably a symptom of your problems rather than the cause – I'd much rather you focused on understanding how your marriage reached this point, learning from your mistakes and becoming the man you'd like to be (rather than someone who I doubt you recognise). Ultimately, you can't make your wife do anything. The only thing you can control – in this out-of-control situations – is your own reactions to the drama (by keeping calm and not turning a crisis into a tragedy).

Returning to your question, I would not tell your wife's lover's wife when you're angry, frightened and desperate. Keep your powder dry (for the time being) and try to be the bigger person rather than descending down to his level.

Why can't I get over her affair? *You're trying to control your wife and her lover when the only things you can truly control are your own thoughts, reactions and behaviour.*

4. After I discovered my husband's infidelity, we went into counselling but he was still writing to her without my knowledge. If I asked anything about the OW, he became so protective of every little detail. It was like pulling teeth getting anything out of him, and at first he would not even let me place a hand on his arm, he was so raw.

The OW is half his age and married with a seven-year-old daughter. Her husband was a gambler and drinker and gambled their rent money, etc. According to my husband they did 'everything except penetrative sex', he says out of respect to her.

He decided to stay with me. We have been through hell. I want him to tell me everything but he will not. She bought him presents but he will not say what they were or if they are still in the house. He will not let me know where they went together to eat, the theatre, etc. I asked him on the back of your book to be transparent with me otherwise I will make the story up. He will not. He says I am torturing him. Should I persist until I know everything?

Andrew writes:

This is tough one. On one hand, you don't want presents from this OW in your house. It seems only kind to let you know what they are and to remove them. On the other hand, he worries that any new piece of information will be used against him (the next time you have a row) or be used to prise yet more details out of his clenched mouth. Both of you are terrified about being stuck but have diametrically opposed ways of resolving it: for you, 'complete honesty', and for him, 'forget everything'.

In my 30 years' experience of dealing with the aftermath of affairs,

I don't think anyone makes a full disclosure at the first attempt. I know all the books and website advice presents this as the gold standard response to being discovered, but real life is seldom so straight forward. The unfaithful partner is just too ashamed to admit to themselves the full extent of the discovery. The discoverer is often overwhelmed with just the idea of the affair – let alone the grisly details – so their other half will tell him or herself it is also kinder to hold back information.

Although your husband sounds more reticent than most men (and women) caught up in infidelity, he is still acting within the bounds of normal. So how do you find a balance between your need to know and his attempts to stop himself from being completely overwhelmed by shame and guilt? My guess is that the subject of the affair only comes up when you are stressed and unhappy, so any conversation starts with a fraught and defensive atmosphere. Meanwhile, when you're doing OK, you keep quiet and simply enjoy the moment.

So let's break the pattern and talk about the affair when you're both calm. Start with everything that's better – so he doesn't get defensive – and thank him for what's he's done that has helped. Next report how you can sometimes feel – the tears, horrible flashbacks, etc – and ask him how he's doing. Finally, ask the crucial question: How do we move forward?

In essence, we need a middle way. You need to ask yourself whether it is possible to know everything about the affair and whether it is desirable too. I have worked with lots of woman who have the main facts – ie, enough to understand the affair and stop it happening again – but accept that they will never be able to climb into their husband's shoes and truly get why he did it. As one client told me: 'It's something I would never do myself and knowing all the facts won't help bridge that gap.' Once you give up on full declaration, you can begin to press for what you truly do need – for example, a ban on any contact with the OW, or a promise to forward any future emails.

Double-check that he thinks he can deliver on these requests. If he can't, then don't set him up for failure.

I think you begin to see how tough this discussion is going to be, but it is possible if you both stay calm. If either of you are beginning to feel overwhelmed take a short break or agree to continue at another agreed time.

Why can't I get over my husband's affair? *You're expecting a full confession but lots of people take months and months to admit to the basic details.*

5. I have been married for 11 years and 2 months. I found out by accident that my wife is in love with another man. I was very hurt but calm and tried to understand her reasons. After weeks of pain she told me everything. She was relieved. While struggling to accept the situation, the guy moved and she cheated on me again. I found out about this by accident as well. I was very understanding because I saw that she was confused and traumatised beyond belief.

Why did she do this? Well for the last three years we have had financial problems and I was blocked in a daydreaming magical auto-solving wishing state. She was, and still is, my sun but I was not able to actually do anything.

During the past three years, slowly but surely, she started feeling like I didn't care at all – until last year she grew so desperate that she let herself fall in love with another man (who she dismissed quickly), then finally settled on someone who is ten years older.

This guy is apparently mature, smart, and above all, very ambitious. They fell in love after a week, then he left the country. She told me that she never thought of the consequences. She just wanted to get away from the payments and the problems. I saw her crying and suffering on many occasions, but I didn't take any notice, and if she had not worked more (12 hours a day) the bank would've taken the house. So all this pressure made her escape into another world.

She tried to tell me that we needed to fix the problem or she would divorce me, but she did not want to hurt me. We are still extremely good friends and have affection up to the sky.

She is now going to France to visit her lover and his family for Christmas, which makes me want to die, of course. On the one hand she is trying to find some major fault with him so she can stop being in love with him, while on the other hand, I suppose, she just can't stop wishing to be around him.

I offered to let her go and divorce her, but she said she can't dump me yet. She said she just can't and if she can see changes in me she would like to try again. (Indeed, her biggest concern seems to be for me to become a man again and take the whole load off her shoulders. She said that she is not worried she won't be able to forget him but rather that the passion between us won't come back.)

I am being supportive. I am sure she is very traumatised by the workload, by my abandonment, by her infidelity, and by much more. I am suffering like a dog and try to ignore the fact that she will not try to be mine again until I deserve her and I have to let that guy be part of her life, for now at least.

My question is: Do I have a chance? I am not a bad man. She can tell you that. I was hoping to get cured from being a very spoiled, immature man, but I learn quickly and I would do anything for her.

Do you think she could come back to me? Can I become the man she needs?

Andrew writes:

When a woman tells her husband 'I love another man' the vast majority give up, throw in the towel and either sit in their corner with their hands on their head (or go on to the Internet to find someone else). Meanwhile, if a husband tells a wife that he's fallen for another woman, nine times out of ten she rolls up her sleeves and sets to work. One thing is for sure: She seldom takes his protestations of love at face value. She thinks, 'He doesn't know her', 'She's only been on her best behaviour' and 'Will it last?'

So what I'm saying is don't be sure it is true love. It's much more likely to be 'something to help me feel better' and because our culture comes down hard on affairs (rightly so, in my opinion) the people involved have to tell themselves it is love – or it looks very cheap and makes them feel dirty. Once the bubble of the affair bursts, and the couple have to face the cold hard reality, it all begins to look a bit different.

While I'm staying positive, you have listened, understood and not attacked your wife (which is to your credit). By doing this, you've gathered a lot of useful information. For example, she could forget him but she REALLY needs for you to change. So you know what you've got to do.

I'm not 100 per cent certain from your letter, what you've done to sort out the financial problems yourself or whether it has just been your wife shouldering all the load. If you've been unable to act, I would suspect that you've been depressed but have hoped that time, your latest magical plan or the weather would lift it. If that's the case, your wife will not understand why you haven't been to the doctors. When she's tired and stressed, she will think that's because you didn't care enough or even you didn't love her. So make an appointment and consider counselling too.

Your wife is more worried about getting back her passionate feelings for you than forgetting the other man – it's something I see all the time. Anger, resentment and exhaustion are really destructive for our libido, but once these emotions are expressed and the partner who has fallen out of love feels heard, the spark normally comes back of its own accord. However, if it doesn't I always stress that love-making is a joint project. It is the responsibility of you both, rather than one or other of you always having to initiate.

Ultimately, the first step to being the man she needs is to believe that you can do it. You've done the hardest bit – keeping calm and listening – so you've laid the foundations.

Why can't I get over her affair? *You need to get your confidence back and believe that you're good enough for her.*

HOW DO I TRUST AGAIN WHEN THE AFFAIR HAS BROUGHT BACK THE PAST?

6. I discovered that my husband had been having an affair prior to our separation in June. We have two wonderful children aged six and three and my husband has always been a great dad to both of them. We decided in December to 'try again' and it was at this time, I found out about the scale of the lies he had been telling me. He had even introduced our two children to this woman without telling me (apparently having met by chance in the park!). We are now back in the family home and he appears to be trying, ie not surgically attached to his phone and providing practical reassurances as to where he is and so on.

Despite our good intentions to repair our marriage, I am overwhelmed by how hurtful his actions have been. Sometimes I look at him and despise him. At other times I feel such love and pride for him. This awful pendulum swings pretty often and results in him shouting and getting angry with me. He states that this affair started as a consequence of how I behaved in our marriage... I suffered extreme Post Traumatic Stress Syndrome following a violent attack nine years previously and perhaps brought all of this into our relationship. He also states I was too needy/dependent on him for support and as the attack was prior to us meeting it was therefore not his problem! I also grew up in an incredibly abusive family and left home just before my 16th birthday, so I have not had any good role models to emulate.

In essence I try so very hard to be a good mum so my children have the best life possible, and despite my husband's lies and deceit I want our marriage to work. He says I am trying to sabotage our relationship by raising the affair as a discussion point. He refuses to attend counselling and will not talk to me about it. So I carry this around with me and simply can't see a way forward. My question then is, Can you love someone you cannot trust? And if you can't trust them, what is the point?

Andrew writes:

Congratulations on recognising the reasons why this is so tough, if you come from an abusive home it is hard to trust in the best of circumstances. You're also likely to try extra hard to be a great mum to compensate for what happened when you were small. Unfortunately you can also exhaust yourself and your marriage, and that might be one of the reasons why your husband felt so helpless and hopeless that he was tempted by an affair. There is another issue that I see, time and again, when someone has had a difficult childhood. You'd think watching your parents torture each other would put you off love forever but it makes you believe it in even more. You want someone to come and rescue you, kiss and make everything better. But your husband is just a regular man – with flaws like everybody else – not a knight in shining armour. So although he might sound cruel when he bats away the attack as 'not his problem', he's simply feeling small and inadequate.

So what are you going to do? I know it all sounds overwhelming but I have one really positive message that I want you to take away. You can save this marriage on your own and the reason for that is – if you can change, you will change the dynamic in the relationship and he will begin to change. If he won't have counselling, go on your own. It will be a chance to talk about past trauma and the post-traumatic stress disorder. You will also learn new ways to process the pain and self-soothe – rather than expecting your husband to rescue you. I know this sounds like a lot of work and sometimes giving up seems the easy option; however, some simple changes can begin a positive cycle where one change for the better encourages another and another.

If you are feeling down over the coming weeks, I'd ask you to 'report' your feelings rather than to go on the attack or create a scene in the hope that your partner will feel guilty and offer reassurance and love. So what do I mean by reporting your feelings? For example, 'I'm feeling sad' or 'the pain is overwhelming'. Your husband can then offer a hug or an apology or simply listen – rather than going on the defensive. In this way, you can move away from the grand inquisition which is pushing your husband away – but still feel that you can talk about the impact of infidelity on you.

Finally, you ask can I love somebody I cannot trust? I'm afraid the answer is yes. We think that love is the answer to all our prayers, that's what all the love songs and the promise of a soul mate suggests. However, love is hard, it takes work, skills and knowledge on how to communicate.

Unfortunately you didn't learn these skills when you were young, but it's never too late. I think you are strong enough to change and learn to be different and that's why I feel more positive than you do.

Why can't I get over his affair? *You need to focus on working on yourself rather than waiting for your partner to change.*

7. Last year I wrote to you about trust issues in my rela-tionship after my partner had an emotional affair and then two years later struck up an inappropriate friendship. Following your advice, I spoke with him and told him how unhappy I was and for the first time he acknowledged the problem. He changed his phone number and cut off contact

with the 'friend' in question. Slowly but surely things have been improving. However, in the past couple of months his parents have split up – initially just temporarily but, due to his father's behaviour since, this has turned into a permanent split. Watching his mum hunt for evidence of other women, and find it, and hearing his dad's excuses have brought bad memories flooding back. I've managed to suppress them until now but I feel almost overwhelmed by thoughts and doubts I hadn't entertained for nearly a year.

I feel terrible because it's nothing my partner has done and I'm panicking because I don't know how to deal with these feelings. Last year I wasn't sure I wanted to stay with my partner because of the lack of trust, but he's been completely open and honest with me; our relationship still isn't at full-strength but I'm prepared to keep working at it. Now I'm fighting the urge to check his emails and phone bills and I'm angry with him for no good reason – I feel like I've been set-back a year. I'm scared to admit to him how I feel because I know how hurt and upset he'll be to be reminded of the past and he's under so much stress with his parents (they have no other relatives).

Andrew writes:

I don't normally answer more than one letter from people (or I'd never have time to write my books) but I thought I would on this occasion as it will give hope to other people that if you face problems they get better.

I'm not surprised that your husband's father's affair has caused so much upset and has set back your recovery. I know you don't want to increase his burden, but if you run away or suppress a problem, it will come back (and bite you on the bum). If you hold back anger, it will pour out as a rant! So let's be proactive. Choose a time when you're feeling calm and he's not too stressed and ask him how he's coping with the fall-out of his parent's split. He most probably will not jump at the opportunity to talk, so have a couple of back-up questions ready. For example, how do you think your mum's coping? Has it been hard listening to your dad? Next, tell him calmly, what it's been like for you. Finally, tell him that you love him and how grateful you have been for all his hard work rebuilding your marriage, and finally ask for a cuddle. It's amazing how a complement or a thank you can change the atmosphere.

So I would focus on improving how you communicate today (rather than going over old ground in the past) and learning to raise issues in a timely manner rather than letting them fester. It is one of the most important lessons to learn from infidelity. Go for it!

Why can't I get over his affair? *You've had an understandable setback. So go back to basics – like improving communication – and don't let it derail your recovery.*

8. Am I allowed to not want to hear about my wife's previous life?

I met my wife at a time when she was pretty damaged by a fairly rough life. No more than usual – just split parents and reduced affection for her. At a young age she had a relationship which she would explain to me was loveless and that she was used, etc. (we'll call this Mr A). Then she got into another relationship for many years, which she also explains was loveless. However this one, Mr B, she got engaged to and was all set to marry when I came along.

We are on our tenth year together, nine years married

with three children. We are a very loving family and moved countries far away from all our previous problems to start again. Then randomly we came across Mr A in a pub! My wife (shaking) almost dropped to the floor with excitement, and exchanged numbers.

I am obviously torn apart by her reaction and would happily end it all if it wasn't for my beautiful children. She deleted Mr A's number from her phone and says she only loves me.

Now, only about four weeks later, people from our home country are clearing out our old house and find a load of my wife's home videos of her with Mr B and her brother who she loves dearly. She's delighted and wants them sent over! Great. How much am I going to enjoy seeing her with someone else again? She says she wants them to remember happy times with her brother at a time of her life where things were hard for her.

I want to feel like my wife is mine; I certainly don't want my kids seeing her being loving to anyone else, on video. I've had enough, I feel destroyed and have lost all my unconditional love for her. I wish I hadn't had my beautiful kids because I could act on my feelings and leave. My wife is constantly loving me and seeking my affection, but I'm struggling to give it now that I don't feel our entire world is just about the two of us and the children.

Andrew writes:

My guess is that you're going to hate my answer. You're going to be angry with me and probably stop reading before you're halfway through. However, I hope that when you've calmed down, you will return and read it properly and, for a while, entertain the idea that some of what I have to say might be true. If you do, you will have a much happier marriage.

Are you a jealous man? It certainly sounds like it from your letter. You want to feel: 'My wife is mine.' But we can't own people. They are not possessions. The entire world cannot be about just you and the children. That is not only suffocating, but when something goes wrong – like now – you feel that your life is over. If you have friends, they can give you a fresh perspective. If you have outside interests – like golf – you can unwind and realise that you might have exaggerated the upset. If you're involved with family – rather than moving country to be away from them – you have support and love in hard times.

I'm also worried that you're putting your interpretation on something and turning it into the gospel truth. For example, she meets an old flame and shaking with emotion drops to the floor. In your mind, this is from passion. It could equally be <u>fear</u> that you are going to make her life a misery.

You are also choosing the most dramatic conclusion. In your mind, these home movies have your wife and Mr B staring into each other's eyes and tiptoeing through fields of flowers while The Carpenters sing 'Close to you'. In reality, it's probably mostly her brother and Mr B eating a burger at a family barbecue in the background. Next, you're upping the stakes by worrying about what your children will think of 'their mother with another man'. Firstly, they don't have to see the videos, if there is anything distasteful (which I doubt). Secondly, they will probably not even notice this man because they'll be looking at how their mother looked before they were born. Finally, if they do think of her and him, it will be a huge joke because your children don't see the world through your eyes.

Rather than trying to control your wife and banish her past, I wonder if you could look at your own past. Why do you find even a home movie threatening? My guess is that deep down you're frightened of losing her. For some reason, you don't feel good enough and have to guard her from everybody else. She loves you and your children. She must be heartbroken about how everything is between you at this moment. So what's gone wrong? My guess is that your parents did not make you feel good about yourself growing up. I wonder if you were abandoned by your dad?

I don't know if you have read this far, but I have one final thought which I hope will help you feel calmer. I call it the 80 / 20 rule. When something is really difficult, it is normally 80 per cent about the past and only 20 per cent about today. Understanding your past will help you concentrate on what is really happening rather than fighting old ghosts.

Why can't I get over her affair? *You need to face the past rather than run away from it.*

WHY WON'T MY PARTNER ANSWER MY QUESTIONS?

9. My wife admitted to an affair that took place for about two years. She would see him when she went home to visit her parents. She has provided details and I feel that she is being honest. However, she said that she had another affair with someone I know. She said that it only happened once and he couldn't get it up. She said they got together in a park. With the first affair, it took her time to tell me the extent (it started as a one-night stand, then later conversations turned into a two-year affair). I caught her having phone sex with the second person, it was very graphic and included comments about times that they had gotten together. I feel she is lying about the extent of this affair because he is here locally and she thinks I might retaliate. How do I get her to open up, so that we can start rebuilding trust and honesty?

Andrew writes:

You need to think long and hard before asking for details about what your wife did sexually with these men. Be certain you truly want to hear these details. Once they have been said – and the picture is in your head – it is going to take a long time to erase it. There is a second reason for getting you to think this through. If you have a sensible reason for wanting to know and can explain it in detail, I think she is more likely to listen and cooperate. So ask yourself: 'How will knowing the details help my recovery?'

Is she still reticent? Share some of your guesses why she could be holding out. Acknowledge your faults – if you really are somebody who is likely to retaliate – but explain why you've decided this wouldn't be a good idea (ie it will let even more people into the secret and just make everything worse). Keep calm as crying or getting angry will make her clam up.

Finally, instead of focusing on the details of the sex acts, you need to understand why your marriage sunk so low that your wife decided to have not one but two affairs – and started having sex in parks! Once you've got a handle on what went wrong, you can start to fix it.

Why can't I get over my partner's affair? *You're focusing too much on what happened and not enough on why.*

10.
How Can I Ever Trust You Again? is fantastic and has cheered me up and given me hope. However, I do need some guidance…

I've known my wife for over 30 years (we grew up together abroad); our relationship turned romantic some 15 years ago, and we have been married for 8 years. I discovered that my wife was having an affair about three weeks ago. She had a previous affair three years earlier but she told me about that one and we 'moved on' from this (or so I thought).

Having confronted her about the latest affair, she denied it at first but once I said I had evidence she then said she was sorry that I had to find out that way. We then tried to talk about why she was unfaithful – she just wouldn't open up to me or tell me anything. I then asked whether she was so deeply unhappy about us that it drove her to do this. She said she wasn't deeply unhappy with us. I then said was it because she didn't enjoy sex? She said no, that sex had been good in the past between us and that I wasn't unattractive – in fact she said that I was the best-looking guy she had had a relationship with! But she did say she was confused and depressed.

I forgave her on the night I found out about the affair. She started crying when I said that she had been forgiven and she said she didn't deserve me and that I was too good for her. We agreed that we should get counselling and try and address why she had been unfaithful again.

She then gave me the 'I love you but' (ILYB) speech and that she was unable to choose between me and her lover, although she had said she ended the relationship (upon my request) soon after I had found out what was going on. She also said that we should perhaps go for a trial separation, but I said that we should not act in haste given that we have a toddler who we both love to bits.

I've expressed my love for her; I have never loved anyone else other than her, and I have given her loads of affection but she isn't reciprocating. Looking back at my behaviour over the first week of the crisis, I felt that this was coming across as needy, desperate and probably deeply unattractive to her (she's not used to me being like this)! So I changed my approach the following week and have done the opposite – no longer saying I love her and only occasionally giving her a hug and a kiss on the mornings when I leave for work, acting happy and positive about things – the strange thing is that some of this is rubbing off on her and she seems to be in a slightly better frame of mind.

What can I do to help her open up to me? What first steps do we need to take?

So far I've tried being loving, going on a romantic dinner in luxurious surroundings, gone salsa dancing (I wasn't so comfortable about this although she was always asking me to go with her), written some short love notes, sent text messages (something I never do), bought her some jewellery and hidden it for her to find it later, but I feel none of this is helping her open up to me.

PS She's halfway through reading your book (which can only be a good sign).

Andrew writes:

I am glad that you have found my book useful and that your wife has decided to read it too. Reading your letter, there are two points that I want to make. The first is about the affair. I am concerned about how quickly you 'forgave' your wife. Partly because in the shock of discovery, it is difficult to know everything, and partly because something given so quickly (and possibly without thinking it through) can be devalued. In reality, the only way to truly forgive is to deal with all the complicated feelings of jealousy and betrayal and to rebuild trust again. In my experience, that takes months not minutes.

So for you to reach forgiveness so quickly, you will have had to suppress and push down all your complicated and dark feelings... and this brings me on to my second point. You sound an incredibly nice person. There is nothing wrong with that – in fact we need more nice people in this world – however, it is possible to be too nice. I find a lot of guys today suffer from the same problem; they will bend over backwards to please their wives and instead of being grateful, the wives lose respect and don't find their husbands particularly sexy!

Why should this be? It's back to not showing your true feelings. If she does something terrible – like cheating, saying she's given up the affair and still carrying on – but you only react deep inside (where she cannot see), she either thinks you do not care, you are a total wimp or that nothing she does (however horrible) moves you. All of these things would make her feel very alone. Getting angry is not only real, and honest, but it shows – in a strange way – that you care.

By all means do nice things for your wife – doing the salsa for her shows you are prepared to go the extra mile – but ask for things in return too. When she says something horrible, don't be silent or turn the other cheek – tell her how you feel. For example, I had a wife who had had an affair and in counselling said it was because 'my husband is getting old, saggy and losing his hair'. He just sat there. I'm not suggesting that you are rude back but saying nothing or being nice is deeply unhelpful.

Up to now, you've been trying to encourage your wife to open up by being nice to her. However, there is a much better way to bring emotions and issues to up the surface, and that's having an argument. Allowing yourself to get angry – and show your true feelings – is an incredibly intimate thing to do. She will probably get angry in response. Great! She'll probably say what she's thinking too and you'll get a real insight into how she's really feeling. An argument will also stop you turning into a doormat. So next time she says something unfair, don't just walk away – stay and fight your case. It will make you feel better and in the long run it will provide a 'realness' rather than 'fake niceness' on to which the two of you can build a good and strong relationship.

Why can't I get over my partner's affair? *You're suppressing your anger.*

11.

Fourteen months ago, I found out my husband was having an affair. We have been married just short of 20 years. We have four beautiful daughters and were travelling well, or so I thought.

From the day I discovered this affair, my husband has promised to end it, then left our home, then returned again to leave after three weeks. This has happened four times.

I have allowed this behaviour as each time I've thought,

'He must be sure this time' and each time I am let down. The longest period of return has been this year and he stayed three months. This last time he returned he spoke about activities we would do together, work around the house. He even went to a counsellor. But once again he left and has returned to the woman he states he loves. Each time he returns, I question my sanity as to why I am allowing this? And then I find I am waiting for him to return again. Why would he constantly lie about what he is doing?

In discovering the affair, I found my husband had told many lies, bought items and hid them. He does not seem the person I knew and loved. Now he has bought a motorcycle upon his last departure. And the OW has never left us alone, even though she knew we were trying to reconcile our relationship.

I am worried that what I am doing is setting my girls up to accept lies, deceit and deception in their own lives. I brought this up in discussion with my husband and he stated that our children had not been affected by our actions. I do not agree with this.

What do I do? How long do I wait? Is he just hedging his bets?

Andrew writes:

When someone lies and cheats, you end up questioning everything because nothing makes sense. So let me try and shine some light into the gloom.

He is probably in such turmoil that he doesn't know what he wants from one minute to the next and I'm afraid that you probably don't help because, quite naturally, you want certainty. So when he talks about coming home, you welcome him with open arms and don't listen to his concerns or fears. Perhaps he does express them but you get angry, tearful or tell him to think about your 'beautiful girls' (and what he's doing to them). Guess what? He squashes down all his feelings and pretends to himself and everybody else that he's certain (that he wants to return), but just pretending the original problems (that make him unhappy and open to the affair) don't exist isn't going to make them go away.

I think you need to understand why men fall out of love. In most cases, it's because they don't feel loved themselves. I know you're going to say but I *did* love him and everything was fine. However, time and time again, men feel their wives leave them first! Your mouth is going to drop on the floor now. Who? How? I've never strayed! However, lots of women become so wrapped up in their children that they neglect their husbands. As some men tell me 'she was too good a mother and not a good wife'. Every time someone talks about their 'beautiful' children, my alarm bells go off because it sounds like they have been put centre stage, and not just adored but idolised. We get married because we enjoy doing things together and want to be together – and then have children and take each other for granted.

In many cases, the men who are torn between two women are also people pleasers (who keep everybody else happy and neglect their needs) and cannot be assertive – by this I mean ask for what they want. For example, can we have more couple time and less family time? If they do drop hints or ask outright, but it doesn't happen, they switch off their disappointment and their resentment (but in doing so risk turning off all their feelings – including love). Unfortunately, there is only so long you can go on ignoring your needs before you snap and say I deserve something for me. (This is where the mistress comes in.)

So why does he keep on lying? He's a people pleaser and he wants to make you happy (when the words are coming out of his mouth). However, he's now trying to please two women and so he's lying twice as much and to everybody (including, most seriously of all, himself). He doesn't know what the hell he wants (and if he's not careful will end up getting seriously depressed or having a breakdown).

So what do you do? You've got to understand this situation better. Ask him 'What went wrong with our marriage?' and 'What could I have done differently?' 'What impact did the children have on our marriage?' and 'Why didn't you feel loved?' Keep the door open for further talks and be pleasant and cooperative over the girls – but tell him you're taking six months out to sort your head out. Once you're both calmer, you'll have a better sense of how to move forward.

Why can't I get over my partner's affair? *You haven't addressed the real reasons for his unfaithfulness and his inability to commit.*

WHAT IF IT FEELS HOPELESS BECAUSE MY PARTNER IS STILL IN CONTACT WITH THEIR LOVER?

12. My husband of 17 years had an affair with a work colleague last year, which got pretty sexual but they did not get to do the deed.

He has always maintained that he loves me and wants our marriage to work; however, the affair continued after I found out. I asked him to leave, which he did for three months and during that time the affair did not continue. He then returned and we are starting to rebuild our marriage.

The OW is now pregnant by her husband. However, she is next in command in the company and my husband maintains that she is the best person he has ever worked with. They have a bond and although he recently resented her, now wants to get past this and continue with their working relationship.

I have told him that their bond makes me uncomfortable and he understands this, but he is planning on taking her for lunch for her annual appraisal. I am starting to feel that the emotional connection has not gone away. How do I communicate this without becoming a dictator? He does not appear to understand this.

Andrew writes:

I let out a great big sigh when I read your letter. I can't tell you how many hours I spend with clients on the issue of appropriate contact with the affair partner after the affair has ended. The situation is made worse by your husband continuing to lie after being discovered. To be honest, I don't think he's still being honest with himself: Why does a work appraisal need to be done over lunch?

So why have you hit this roadblock? I think it is for one of three possibilities, or possibly some combination:

1. *You haven't explained your case properly.* I have to say 'uncomfortable' would not describe my feelings, more exasperation, annoyance and a dash of anger: How can he expect to have a close working bond with this woman after he betrayed your marriage? Maybe you've been so keen to save your marriage that you've not been entirely honest about how much you've been hurt, or did not lay down clearly the conditions for him to return – especially regarding ongoing relations with the OW. What would happen if you were honest? This does not mean you dictate but that you explain clearly the impact on you, what is acceptable and what isn't (if he wishes to stay married).

2. *He doesn't feel heard.* In his mind, he has a good case for continuing as before and if only you would listen, he could talk you round to his way of thinking. So ask him to explain, in detail, how the 'business' relationship with the other woman will work, what would be the boundaries between allowable contact and tipping back into an affair? Don't interrupt, get upset or contradict, just let him lay everything out and ask questions to get clarification.

3. *The two of you don't know how to negotiate.* The solution is probably not going to be you having your way (she leaves the company and never speaks to him again) or his way (they can continue their friendship as if nothing happened) but somewhere in between. What is stopping you from finding a compromise that would be acceptable to both of you? My guess is that you're trying to rush through the discussion – because it's painful – but one of my key maxims is 'We need to explore and understand before we act.'

So keep asking questions, keep talking and sharing your feelings. Ultimately, I hope he'll decide for himself where to draw the line, so it will be somewhere he can deliver, but somewhere that makes you feel safe too.

Why can't I get over my partner's affair? *It takes time to negotiate a way forward that's acceptable to both of you.*

13. I have just been through the ILYB conversation with my wife and, of course, it came as a total shock. I discovered that she had been having an 'inappropriate relationship' with a divorced man via email and text and they had been contacting each other four or five times a day for the past three months. However, when this all came out, she said how unhappy she was (we have been married for 15 years) and that is why she had kept this relationship secret. It was flirty but, as yet, I do not think anything has happened between them.

The problem is that although this is now out in the open, and I understand that it is a result of her unhappiness, despite my efforts she is unwilling to give up the relationship. They continue to text, phone and email and she is adamant that as there is nothing going on, she has nothing to apologise for. I feel that we cannot deal with this (and we have three children under ten) without her putting some distance between her and him. I already feel shocked and hurt and this just makes me feel even more insecure and anxious. I don't feel she can be committed to resolving our problems (despite saying so) without admitting the other relationship is wrong and a problem. She seems more interested in saving this relationship than ours and just today I discovered (despite her promise to be open about contact with him) that they had spent an hour on the phone to each other, but she will not reveal what they talk about.

I cannot sleep or eat, but she is not interested yet in the things I have been doing to try and improve things – including being completely honest about how I feel and what I want to do together to put things right. Your book, *How Can I Ever Trust You Again?* is great and very perceptive about a lot of our issues but does not give any advice for a situation like this. Trust has gone between us, she is defensive and I'm suspicious, and I feel she says one thing but acts in a different way. I do not want to give her an ultimatum or distress the children, but I cannot carry on like this. I love her with all my heart, but at the moment I just feel pitied and I cannot go on like that. My wife is obsessed with another man. Any advice welcome....

Andrew writes:

Affairs and inappropriate relationships are smokescreens that stop the person concerned from having to face their day-to-day problems. So although it is easy – and very understandable – to obsess about this man, it is important to remember that he is a symptom of the problem and not the cause.

Having said that, your wife's obsession with this man is deeply unhelpful. It would be much better for everyone's happiness if she spent an hour talking to you! So what's stopping her? My guess is that it is one of two possible scenarios. Firstly, you have been so anxious to save your marriage, so keen to avoid conflict that you have been playing 'Mr Nice Guy' and she has not truly taken on board how miserable this is making you. Obviously anyone with two eyes would be able to tell that Mr Nice is upset, but she is blinded by her obsession with this guy and chooses not to see. If this is the case, you need to be more open and honest and show your anger. It will be messy and unpleasant but she will not be able to pretend that her relationship is just a harmless friendship.

Alternatively, you have become so angry – almost bouncing off the walls – that she has been able to write your reaction off as 'over the top' and 'unfair' and therefore, in her mind, she is absolutely justified in going her own sweet way. If this is the case, you need to approach her in a calm and reasonable manner. Rather than demanding to know what she's been talking about, ask her to explain why she is so unhappy. Don't interrupt with explanations, justifications or promises to make it better. Just listen. Nod and ask her for more details. (If you are tempted to interrupt, dig your nails into the palm of your hands or bite the inside of your cheeks.) When you've listened to her side, she will be ready to hear your message: This 'friendship' is stopping us from moving forward. Whichever approach, I would focus on things between you and her. It is pointless debating whether this relationship is right or wrong or whether she 'has anything to apologise for'. The issue is: How do you repair your relationship? Leave it up to her to draw the obvious conclusion.

If this does not work, my other thought is that affairs thrive on secrecy. In this private world, the person who is deceiving does not have to face up to the impact of her or his behaviour. So I would bring this 'friendship' out into the open. Speak to her mother, for example, explain the problems and ask for advice. It will provide you with some emotional support and she will probably have a private word with her daughter.

Why can't I get over my partner's affair?

It's still going on.

14.

We had so many issues over our seven years together including problem daughters from a previous marriage, Child Support Agency mistakes, work issues, health issues and money worries. Most of which have been dealt with, but the result was that I became down, demotivated and our love life suffered.

My wife briefly moved out early this year, so I left and she returned to the house. She has now recently found somewhere else to live and I am back in the house. In the meantime, we had spells of getting on and I heard positive things from her, only for me to push her away and to say no.

Recently she agreed to counselling and said she would not contact anyone who she thought I saw as a threat. This included an old flame that was on the scene between her prior relationships, but with who she had no contact with until Easter when she contacted him online against my wishes. She then continued to have contact via texts after deciding not to. It also included a friend of mine who took her side and 'used' to like her, although she has no feelings towards him.

After a couple of sessions she decided to invite the friend over. I reminded her of what she said and she told me she'd changed her mind, but will not leave counselling even if I do. The other night she tried to convince me that there would be no harm in contacting the old flame too. Other people have caused problems and delayed the process of healing in the past months and I do not wish this to happen again. Her old diary also stated that she loved this guy, etc, and she mentioned him on only a few occasions in our first year together. I always suspected she would run to him if we had problems. Well, this time she did. I want her to leave the past in the past. She tells me there is nothing in it and she isn't attracted to him.

She also tells me that she does not love me but is trying to see where the sessions go and she needs to understand herself first, which could take months or years. Yet my body clock is ticking, my father was only ten years older than I am today when I lost him. I am not the most patient of people and have had nearly four months of this.

Why does my wife contact her ex? Why must she make this a problem when we have so many others to solve?

Andrew writes:

I know it's painful to not only struggle to save your marriage but also worry that your wife secretly loves someone else. So you have my unreserved sympathy. However, your solution at the moment is to cross-question her which just PUSHES HER AWAY. Alternatively, you tell her who she can speak to or not (it does sound like an order rather than a request) and this just PUSHES HER AWAY. You've become obsessed with the other man and getting him out of the picture. (In your letter I've not heard one thing that that you're going to counselling to change.) Unfortunately, this obsession with the immediate problem – rather than the root cause – just PUSHES HER AWAY. And to complete the picture, you're not a patient man!

The problem is that this is going to take time and a deeper understanding. Women normally only allow other men to chat them up if they're feeling lonely, desperate and sad. I wonder if you've ever listened to your wife, asked questions and tried to step into her shoes, rather than try to fix things or promise everything is going to be better in the future.

So next time you're tempted to push and get a quick solution which just PUSHES HER AWAY, tell yourself: These men are just a symptom of the problem and the problem is something I've been doing wrong (clue: Not being patient?). I know this is a harsh conclusion but I hope it will empower you.

Start by learning what's gone wrong, understand why you're not a patient man and see if you can fix that. If you can fix that, everything else drops into place.

Why can't I get over my partner's affair? *In the rush to resolve your problems, you have been pushing your wife away, which has increased your anxiety and compounded the problem further.*

15. I have been married for eight years and knew my husband for four years before we got married. We have two children. Our son is five years old and our daughter is two. My husband has been having an affair for the last year with his college ex-girlfriend. They have been in touch with each other even before that on Facebook.

She lives in another country and has been married for three years. My husband goes on business trips to the same country frequently. The last two trips (each 10–12 days long) they were staying together in a hotel. She got pregnant. But, she had the child aborted. My husband told me the story on a very superficial level. Most of the details I found out… and he just kept lying about it till I showed him all the proof. Now hopefully everything is out there.

He thinks he is in love with her even after so many years. She was his first love and he just cannot forget her. At the same time he says he cares for me and the children and can't make up his mind either way.

I have known everything for the past two months. They are still in touch with each other on a regular basis through messages, emails and calls. He cries at home… asks me to forget everything…feels bad that he is making me go through all this.

But still he is not able to decide anything for good. I feel that I can't take the 'insult to injury' on a daily basis. If we didn't have children the decision would have been a little bit easier for me. I don't want to be impulsive on this one, but at the same time it is increasingly difficult for me to continue like this.

You obviously have seen lots of cases similar to mine. I want to know what happens in most of these cases. Does the unfaithful spouse realise his/her mistake? Do they come back to their senses? Do they realise the grass looks greener on the other side? And most importantly, what I should be doing at present?

Andrew writes:

Yes, I have seen loads of cases similar to yours and I will be 100 per cent honest: I can't predict what your husband will do... because a lot of it will depend on how you act. However, I have some general observations.

1. *Most affairs self-destruct.* They are built on fantasy and secrets and when they see the cold light of day implode.

2. *Old flames affairs are more durable.* There is less fantasy and people tell themselves 'we were meant to be together'.

3. *Women find it almost impossible to forgive their partners after an abortion.* Even though they walk into the clinics using their own legs and sign the consent form with their own hands. They blame the man for not stopping them or for making them do it, or some combination of both.

4. *Having two children under five has a serious impact on a couple's sex lives.* For the first 18 months after a baby is born all the oxytocin – the bonding hormone – goes into the relationship between the

mother and child. Just when she has recovered, she has a second child! It doesn't mean that you're not sexually responsive but that you need to be wooed and coaxed into love-making. Sadly, some men think their wife doesn't love them any more and look elsewhere for consolation.

5. *It will probably take somewhere between a year and two years to recover from this affair.* It will take a lot of work (on both your parts). He will need to grieve for his lost 'love' and you will need to grieve for the 'innocent' relationship that you had before.

6. *Couples with children are more likely to survive an affair than those without.* It helps people find a balance between satisfying individual short-term goals (in his case to feel better today by contacting the ex or in your case fleeing the marriage to feel safe) and considering others and the greater good.

Ultimately, I think the future is in your hands. If he was leaving he would have left by now. If he did leave and go to her, the recriminations would tear them apart within weeks (and he'd be back). To be honest, I think he sounds rather weak and is waiting for you to make your mind up. That's why I think you should start reading around this topic, thinking and reflecting. Don't rush into making a decision or keep off-loading on to your friends because they will want to advise and unless they've been in the same position will not truly understand. Ultimately, it's your life and only you can decide what's best for you.

Why can't I get over my partner's affair? *You're still deciding which way to jump and that's fine because it is better to make a considered rather than an impulsive decision.*

HOW CAN I RECOVER FROM DOUBLE BETRAYAL: MY PARTNER *AND* MY BEST FRIEND?

16. Three weeks ago my suspicions that my husband of 12 years was having an affair with my friend were confirmed when I saw them together. At first he cried and said it was a one-off and that he wanted to stay with his family, which was what I wanted too, but over the next few days I found out he had lied and that the affair has been going on for at least six months. He says it only ever involved kissing; I'm not sure I believe him. He asked if I wanted him to go to his mother's, which I did as I needed to cope with my emotions, not just about the betrayal, but also the lying after they were discovered. He then told me ILYB (which is how I came to read your book, *I Love You But I'm Not in Love With You*) and that he needed space. I was prepared initially for him to come home and get some help but he refused.

Two weeks ago we told our children aged 10 and 11 that he wouldn't live with us anymore. My husband has seen a personal counsellor but we haven't had a proper conversation together yet – each time I ask he makes up an excuse, too tired, we'll only argue, etc. I can see from reading *ILYB* all the mistakes we have made along the way – not arguing (he would always walk out), not making time for each other, the book is almost written about us! I accept my share of the blame for the problems, although not for the affair, which he says was my fault!

The problem now is that I feel empowered by the situation; his leaving has made me take control of my whole life and although I don't want to give up on the relationship I need my husband to stop being the victim and address the issues. He has booked an appointment with a couple's counsellor this week and I am prepared to go with him. The children have been amazing and although I miss him, I don't feel that I need him any more. Everything is happening now on his terms and I find this annoying, he hasn't once asked how I or the children are coping. He seems like a different person from the man I love and I don't know what to do.

Andrew writes:

If infidelity was not painful enough, there are circumstances which take the heartache and effectively quadruples it. For example, discovering your partner is cheating with a close friend, or even worse – someone from your family (or extended family). Not only has your partner, who you thought had your best interests at heart, betrayed you but a friend who you also trusted. Your mind races through all the times that you offered hospitality and opened up your heart and home to this woman and you feel completely violated.

I wouldn't be at all surprised if you've been asking: Why from all the millions of women in the world has he chosen to be unfaithful with this one? Unfortunately, people tend to 'fall in love' with someone with whom they have repeated exposure – which is normally someone at work but can also be from a circle of friends. You'd think that the 'lovers' would realise they were about to cross a boundary and step back but our culture has all sorts of unhelpful myths that facilitate affairs. For example, 'love will find a way' (and somehow nobody will really be hurt) and 'this is bigger than both of us' (so we don't have to take responsibilities for our actions). I will stop lecturing because it does nobody any good (or makes anybody change their mind). However, I do hope it makes you realise what you're up against and stops you being too self-critical.

I'm interested that you write that the 'problem' is that you feel 'empowered'. I think a lot of people would consider that the saving grace! So I wonder what the 'problem' might be? After such an extreme betrayal, it is very common to shut down, pull up the drawbridge and protect yourself. It would certainly allow you to 'take control' of your life, but it also stops you listening to your husband (or trying to understand him). So he's a 'different man' from the one you married and, not surprisingly, as this man has hurt you so profoundly, you don't know if you want to be with him. However, looking a bit deeper at what's going on might help you understand him and your dilemma.

Let's start by asking: Why do men (or women, for that matter) turn into strangers to their partners who thought they knew them so well? The men and women who have affairs are often people pleasers. They want to make others happy and they want to be liked. So far so good. However, what happens when their needs, wants and desires clashes with those of their partner. Normally, they swallow these desires and tell themselves 'my needs don't matter'. In the language of assertiveness, they are being passive (because they consider their needs, wants and beliefs to be of lesser importance than everybody else's). However, there is only so long you can go on downgrading your needs before you start to think, 'I deserve this' and 'What about me?' At this point, people pleasers turn 180 degrees and become incredibly selfish. In the language of assertiveness, they are being domineering (because their needs, wants and beliefs are of supreme importance and damn everybody else). If your husband has gone from being passive to domineering, he will seem like a very different person! However, I would hope – instead of alternating between passive and domineering – he would become assertive. This is where both people's needs are important and when there is a clash, the couple learn to negotiate.

I wonder if there is another reason why your husband seems

different. The German philosopher Nietzsche called marriage the 'grand dialogue', by which he means we have to keep talking and remain curious about each other. Unfortunately, lots of couple abandon this conversation and substitute it with shorthand (so they don't properly explain themselves), imagine that they 'know' each other (can we ever know someone; can we even know ourselves?) and the interchange is reduced to giving or receiving instructions from each other. (At this point, do a couple have a marriage or simply a business arrangement to bring up children?) Could your husband have become a stranger and able to dismiss you so easily because you've both stopped talking and listening to each other? In which case he might seem a different man from the man you married, but 12 years and two children has changed him – and you.

So I suppose I'm saying it's fine to be empowered and decide that his betrayal has been too great, and you want to end the marriage. However, you have two children together, so I would hope that you keep listening to him, trying to understand his point of view and to negotiate when, as they most surely will, your needs clash. In this way, you will teach your children an important lesson about good communication. Who knows, it may also help you find a way through this madness and to restore your love for each other.

Why can't I get over my partner's affair? *You've both stopped talking and listening to each other.*

17. My husband and I have been married for 26 years, together for 30+ years; yes, we are childhood sweethearts I suppose. We have two wonderful kids, obviously all grown up now. I had the ILYB speech last year. He said it was down to trust issues, the fact that I had been keeping things from him about the kids. Nothing major, I have lent them money to help them out and not told him – at the time the relationship between him and our son was very strained. I used to be piggy in the middle between them and it was painful to see and hear. My husband basically wanted me to report back to him every time our son did something wrong and the atmosphere was awful. I thought trying to smooth things over between them would help their relationship; obviously not.

Anyway, back to the ILYB… he suggested we take it one day at a time and see where it takes us. We carried on as normal, going out with friends, etc, but the physical side to our relationship seemed to be happening less and less.

Last year, my husband's brother died suddenly (48). It was a massive shock to everyone. He seemed to take everything on, looking after his brother's wife and kids, being there for his sister and his parents. But as he was doing this, he became more and more distant from me and our family. I understand him being there for everyone but he didn't seem to be grieving or opening up to anyone. He's never been one for showing his emotions, a typical man's man as they say, but I'm used to that.

We took our summer holiday, this year as planned, and it was fine. Still no physical stuff though, but I was prepared to wait and not force the issue. On returning he became even more distant from me and began confiding in his sister. To cut a long story short, the decision was made to end our marriage. It was very one sided, I was willing to fight tooth and nail to save it but he was adamant it was over. He said he had tried for 18 months to work out the issues about what I had done and he couldn't trust me any more; no marriage guidance nothing, it was done…

I was, and still am, devastated. I tried not to be negative around him, I tried to carry on as normal as we had agreed to stay together in the house until it had been sold and that things would remain amicable between us.

As time went on, he became like a stranger to me, just me; anyone else saw the same person. His resentment ground me down so much that I am now having counselling as I feel like a failure. In the back of my mind I always thought there was something not quite right. I recently discovered, by ways of his mobile phone account, that he had been in regular contact with a close friend of mine. I tracked his bills back over two years and yes they were texting even then. It was constant, morning, noon and night. This is the friend that we had socialised with, her husband too, had been on holiday with, even the last one, and I had confided so much in. I even work with her. Last month alone there were 1,707 texts just to her number, not to mention numerous calls.

I challenged him and he denied being in contact with her. He continued to blame me for the failure of our marriage. I didn't admit to seeing the bills straight away but eventually I couldn't take it anymore and showed him what I had seen. He still denied it even though it was there in black and white. I can't believe how anyone could be so cruel and devious.

I researched on the Internet and found information on emotional affairs and it ticks all the boxes. How stupid have I been? I caught them texting before and they both said nothing was going on and they would stop.

She has now split up from her husband, divorced in April, and the story is that my husband and her have been out on a few occasions and have kissed, that's all; he said he couldn't take it any further while we were still under the same roof, he wouldn't do that to me. Our kids both hate the situation and say they will never accept them as a couple – as do hers.

I have confronted my husband and he denied constant

contact with her, and he still adamantly blames me for the failure of our marriage. I have even shown him what I discovered, to which he replied that they were just friends.

This is how sick it gets: I'm in the spare room as I am typing this and my husband is in what was our room and he's texting her. Every opportunity when he's on his own he's contacting her. He now says they have been seeing each other only since May. I'm devastated. I still love him…

At work, I have been calm and dignified in her presence but can't help feeling this woman is having a good laugh behind my back. Help! What should I do next?

Andrew writes:

It's never too late to understand about relationships and get the best out of a horrible situation. The problem is that you have a lot of long-term problems that have not been properly attended to over many years. On their own, each one of these is not too bad – in fact every couple deals with them – but the cumulative effect is like rowing from Land's End to New York and being just a degree off course and ending up in Canada.

So what's being going on? Before I start, let me tell you where I stand. Your husband's behaviour is appalling. If he was so unhappy, he should have said something and you could have sorted it out together. So although I have a lot to say to him, he thinks he's found the answer to his prayers (in this OW) and he's not listening. Meanwhile, you're typing in the spare room and I have your undivided attention. So although, I am going to ask you to change – I believe that problems are 'six of one and half a dozen of the other'.

So how did it start to go wrong? I wonder if you've put so much energy into raising your children that you lost sight of each other. He should have spoken up, and indeed he might have tried, but you were too busy or he felt you would not have listened anyway – giving the money to your son, for example. Meanwhile, you have not confronted problems but allowed yourself to be piggy in the middle. If you can talk, it's amazing what you can sort out.

However, not only did your husband not speak up, you did – to someone else. Instead of telling your husband about the problems in your marriage, you've spoken to this 'friend'. What does that change beyond feeling better for a moment? Most probably, you were betraying him by telling intimate secrets to a third party (who he would meet socially). Sadly, it's a situation I see over and over again. Not only did your marriage stay off course but you handed this snake the keys to your husband's heart!

Into this delightful mix, we have bereavement – and your brother-in-law was really young – which often makes the people left behind decide that life is too short to be unhappy and becomes the catalyst for change. Unfortunately, when life is bleak we can reach for an instant solution and someone telling us we're wonderful is like nectar to bees. Before too long, your husband has 'feelings' for the OW and you know the rest. The lovers plough on regardless of the devastation all around them. It's easy to criticise but that will get you nowhere.

Finally, we come to what do you do next? You love him, he wants nothing more to do with you and is blinded by his new love. You have two options: to try to heal and move on or withdraw, bide your time and try to win him back (once he's realised she is not the answer). Fortunately, the first step in both these strategies is the same: understanding how you got into this hole. Sadly, I don't think you have even begun to start this task. You describe your behaviour as 'nothing major', but giving money behind his back is violating a financial boundary and sets up a sub-alliance with your son. Staying with the subject of boundaries, it's fine to share the headlines of the complexity of being married with friends – because it helps us realise that relationships are difficult and we're not the only ones struggling – but it is easy to cross the line and over-share. In this way, we tell our friends too much detail and it becomes a sort of betrayal. I have chosen the words 'boundary' and 'betrayal' for a reason, because it echoes what he has done.

With extreme betrayal, it's easy to focus on the destruction caused by the other party and ignore your part. However, if you learn nothing from this horrible situation, you risk being trapped and feeling bitter (and making it harder for your children to move on). Similarly, if you feel you've done nothing wrong and therefore have no need to change, then your husband won't believe that your marriage can be different either and even if his new 'love' falters he won't return and give your marriage another try.

Why can't I get over my partner's affair? *You have been so busy criticising his behaviour that you have downgraded or overlooked your own contribution to this crisis.*

18. I have purchased two of your books, *I Love You But I'm Not In Love With You* and *How Can I Ever Trust You Again?* They are both great and helping me. I found out that my husband of almost seven years was having an affair with my cousin's girlfriend for about four months. I was devastated when he left to be with her. About three weeks later, when it came time to sign the divorce papers, he said he couldn't lose me and the kids and came home. Well, about three weeks later, I found out that he never stopped seeing her. So again the divorce papers came out and again he couldn't sign and said he would cut her out of his life. I felt OK with this because he did so over the phone while I listened.

Well, about four days went by and she contacted him

begging him to be with her. So again he said he wanted a divorce, and again I got the papers out while he packed. This time when he was getting ready to leave I told him we had to sit our kids down to tell them that he was leaving. He again broke down and couldn't leave. He said he would never answer her calls or emails again. So far, whenever she has tried to contact him, he calls me right away and tells me. This makes me feel that he is trying but I'm scared that he will give in to her again.

The issue is he has such strong feelings for her and says he loves her, that he doesn't know how to get over her. I tell him I will do whatever it takes, that it's only been about a week since the last divorce scare and him cutting her completely off. The first few days were great. I felt like he loved me again but the last couple of days he has become distant once again. He says he is not trying to be but that he just worries about her and is having a hard time getting over her. I don't know what to do. I hate knowing my husband has feelings for some-one else. I also hate feeling like I can just wake up one day and he will say he wants to leave again to be with her. I know we can work it out if he just gets over her. He tells me over and over that he doesn't want to lose me – he's just stuck in the middle. I don't know how long I can take this fear of him leaving me for someone else. What should I do to help him get over her? How do I show him that my love is enough?

Andrew writes:

The emotional turmoil seeps through every line of your letter. You must be exhausted from living on adrenaline and your nerves. You love your husband with every fibre of your body and you are terri-fied of losing him. However, you need to take a deep breath, get a hug from someone who cares deeply for you (like your dad) and trust me, you will survive and – with a bit of luck, wisdom and some compassion for your husband – get though this horrible mess and smile again.

So here goes. First of all, you're making everything more dramatic than it needs to be. I can almost hear the gut-wrenching music as you give him the pen to sign the divorce papers and tell him to explain why he's leaving to the children (and sending them into the cold snow and a life in the workhouse). I am exaggerating but if you read the letters from other people in your situation, you will see that they have not used such emotional language or gestures designed to pull at their partner's heart strings. I know you are going to say that desperate situations require desperate measures, but you're just adding to the drama. Under such pressure, people do stupid things and this is why your husband told you he'd ended the affair but couldn't follow through.

When the infidelity involves someone in your family, the tragedy naturally moves up a couple of notches. While most people don't know the spouses of the affair partner, your cousin is probably phoning you up and giving you updates from his end. Everybody else in the family is more likely to know and form a chorus of opinions, advice and side-taking. If your cousin gets back with his girlfriend, you risk meeting her at big social events with everybody watching from the sidelines. If your husband stays he will have to face your family with everybody knowing exactly what he's done. So if you've been giving family members blow-by-blow accounts of the past few weeks, I would look for support from friends or pour your feelings into a diary. In this way, your life is less likely to descend into a soap opera with other people provoking you into 'something must be done' when in times of high crisis it's better to do nothing. The best time to act is when you're calm, collected and can think everything through.

Finally, I want to give you a big hug myself after reading the final line of your letter. Of course, your love is enough! You don't need to convince him of that. He needs to convince you that he has the strength of character to deserve your love. So stop looking for the perfect line or the magical gesture that will resolve all this mess and instead ask for the strength to sort this out, day by day, week by week because if you learn the lessons from his affair, you will emerge out the other side with a stronger and better marriage.

Why can't I get over my partner's affair? *Everybody else in the family is involved, pumping up your distress and making it harder to see what's really happening.*

HOW CAN I RECOVER WHEN THE AFFAIR HAS GONE ON FOR SO LONG?

19. We are so happy that we have your book *How Can I Ever Trust You Again?* to work on our deep crisis. It helped us a lot. Our states improved, we are very much in love, but I still have severe problems. My husband and I have been a couple for 43 years, since we were teenagers. We had a wonderful time with lots of development; we're married and have two lovely children that are grown-up now.

Twenty years ago he had his first love affair, which I can understand now. It was the first time in years that he had a job abroad and didn't have any other duties than the job during a beautiful summer, and a wife (me) that was very stressed in her job. I think we have learnt a lot since then. Some months ago, I learnt that my husband had again had an affair, for more than *seven* years! During all that time I felt happy and close to him. There were a few slight hints, though, that there might have been something wrong, but my husband never admitted that.

After the affair was no longer secret, we talked a lot and have been very open. He took the decision to stop, and I used your advice to trust him 100 per cent for two weeks. After this it was like a honeymoon period. But in fact he kept in contact and still slept with her at least once. I talked to both of them. His girlfriend said that she needed time to get over the separation, and he said that he couldn't let her go yet. We still took the decision to stick together as a couple because we love each other a lot, but, of course, this was much more difficult than before. He always said that he loved me and that he never wanted to separate from me. And he said that he was always happy with me, that his love for the OW had developed from the job, the time that they spent together and that he was attracted to her because she was a person who was different from me.

It'd be much easier for me if I had reasons, knew what I hadn't fulfilled or where I went wrong. It hurts me so that he lied to me so deeply, and the problem I have is how can I find out if he tells me the truth or not? Do you think that I just need some more time to heal, because it was the second affair, because the affair took place for such a long time and that he lied after he told me that he was going to stop it?

Everything feels so good, but still there are times when I'm so scared. We can talk about my problems, he gives me whatever time I need to talk and is very patient. Have you got any idea what I could do to overcome these insecure feelings?

Andrew writes:

I'm glad that my book has helped because it sounds like you've been through a truly horrible time. I think it is a real tribute to your character that you are not angrier with your husband – but more about that later.

Let's start with your questions: Why didn't you fulfil him enough and therefore manage to prevent him from having the affairs? I think you are expecting rather a lot of yourself. In fact, I don't think anybody – however dedicated to their partner – can fulfil them. Ultimately, I think we are all responsible for making our own life purposeful and worthwhile. (Unfortunately, we think the latest car, ticket for the must-see show, a glass of champagne or – in your husband's case – a bit of sex on the side – will fill us up. More often that not, we're just throwing rubbish into a void.) Basically, it's your husband's responsibility to fulfil himself not yours. All you've got to ask is what makes *my* life meaningful and am I pursuing it – quite a tall order in itself!

So why does it hurt so deeply and why do you need more time to recover? You've answered this next question yourself. Of course, it takes more time to recover from a second affair and especially as he kept on seeing and sleeping with the OW after he was discovered and supposedly trying to save his marriage. Also, the longer the affair, the harder it is for the 'lovers' to break it off (and the longer the mourning takes). I have to say I'm not surprised that they had an 'encore' love-making session. Lots of men, caught in the middle of two women, want to let the OW down gently. Sometimes, they even hope they can 'wean' her off them by slowly reducing contact. I've no idea where they get the idea that this might be a pain-free exit (or that such a thing exists). It just prolongs the agony – for everybody! However, I suppose as these men imagined an affair would be a pain-free way of solving their unhappiness, they are going to be similarly deluded about the endings.

As for your insecure feelings, I think they are perfectly natural and I don't think you should try and overcome them. You need them! They are telling you: he lied and lied again and he could do it again. (Incidentally, I'm not sure where you got the idea that I think you should trust again 100 per cent – trust returns right at the *end* of the process not shortly after discovery. By all means, TRY and give the benefit of the doubt at this point, but that's a long way from trust.)

Summing up, I've got one final thought about how to move forward (beyond what I've already said about not expecting too much of yourself too soon) and that's how I started: Anger. Sometimes we need to get angry. It blasts through the niceness, gets things said that need to be said and changes things. Have you been suppressing your anger? Did your family tell girls that it was not acceptable or ladylike, because my gut feeling is that anger could be your friend?

Why can't I get over my partner's affair? *The longer and more serious the affair, the longer it takes to recover and the better your communication needs to be.*

20.

Last year I found out, by reading an email, my husband of 32 years had been having an affair for over four years. They met while he was travelling abroad for a few weeks to start a job. They met on a city tour bus when he says she came to sit with him. They spent the rest of the day together and she gave him her phone number. The following day, he phoned her, and two weeks later after a number of phone calls and emails, they met up again in another city and spent the weekend in a hotel. He says he only did this because she asked him to phone her and she wanted to meet up again. She asked him to book a hotel, which he did; he thought they might be making love, so he bought Viagra as he was nervous. He says he realised he did not want to do this and doesn't know why he did, but she forced him into making love and he never enjoyed it!!! At the airport when he was leaving they promised to keep in touch and he again phoned her the following day.

They kept in touch by email and phone and the following year they met again in Brazil where she lives and had a beach holiday. Again he says he doesn't know why he went because he had no feelings for her and again she forced him into making love and he never enjoyed it. They still kept in touch and met again two years later. They spent the weekend in Toronto and again he doesn't know why he went thousands of miles to be with someone he didn't want to be with, and again she forced him, etc.

In the email I found, he wrote that 'he couldn't wait until we are together' and he 'loved and missed' her. He told me he'd only sent it because that is what he thought she wanted to hear. He said at first he had loved her, for over three years, and then changed it to he 'thought' he loved her, then he had never loved her, and telling me he loved her was a mistake. He says he has never kissed, hugged or touched her in an affectionate way and that the love-making was because she forced him and he did what he had to, to get it over with, and that it was mechanical and he never once enjoyed it.

He says she was pushing him to live together but he didn't know what to do, but now says that was a mistake as he never wanted to live with her and he had always told her this. We went to Relate [the UK's leading couple counselling charity], but the lady told me she didn't think he would ever tell me the truth and suggested I leave him. He says it was because she didn't like him.

He has always been a kind and loving husband with what I believed a strong moral belief. He is very hard-working with a very confident, strong nature. Now he wants us to try and put this all behind us to make the marriage work (I always thought it did). I asked to be there when he finished the affair but the first time I left the house he said he phoned to finish it.

He insists he doesn't know why he let the affair go on for over four years, although they only met up three times – ten days in all. He can't explain why he would phone, email and go to meet someone he did not want to see. He says he was a reluctant party to the relationship and she was bossy, pushy and demanding, but he only said this after our daughter-in-law said that Brazilian women can be bossy, pushy and demanding! He seems to accept no responsibility; he just admits to what he has done but can't explain why.

Our son refuses to speak with his father and will not have him in his life. Is there any hope?

Andrew writes:

It must have been a horrible shock to discover that the infidelity, that it went on for so long and worse still, that your husband seems to have got so little pleasure out of it. When a partner can't explain the causes of their infidelity, it can be doubly painful and make it *seem* impossible to move forward. After all, if you can't get to the root causes, how can you stop it happening again? So let me try and shed some light on the situation:

1. Some men are not used to analysing their feelings. They just act and therefore find it hard to explain their actions in any circumstances. Does your husband fall into this category?

2. When the affair bubble has burst, and the Discovered looks back on what happened through cool detached eyes – his or her behaviour makes little sense even to him or her. The Discovered comes to the horrible conclusion that it all meant nothing.

3. The British, and in particular the middle class, don't like to upset or let people down, which means they can get into the strange situation of being expected to do something and are too embarrassed to say no. So they sort of go along with things. I know he has let you down, but in his brain, he had divided you and the OW into two separate worlds and believed his actions in one had no effect in the other.

4. He is frightened of saying too much, in case he drops himself even deeper into trouble.

The next issue is that he doesn't seem to 'accept any responsibility' for what happened. This seems like a huge stumbling block to healing but let's look at why he might be like this. When people ask me 'What causes affairs?' I provide this formula:

Problem + poor communication + temptation = Affair

You're not responsible for his problems or resisting the temptation, but you are one half of the communication, so you have to take
some responsibility here. Why was your husband unhappy? Why
couldn't he tell you? How come you didn't hear him, if he did try to
tell you? What I'm saying is that although he is responsible for the
cheating, you are both responsible for the state of the marriage.

It is possible that your husband thinks he is being asked to shoul-
der *all* the blame (although I hate the idea of blame as it gets couples
nowhere). When you are able to look at your part and accept your bits
of this train crash situation, he will be more likely to take on his share.

At the moment, I see your marriage as a bit like the problems in
Northern Ireland (before the Good Friday Agreement). There are
two sides – both deeply unhappy and angry but unable to put aside
their problems for long enough to start really talking. However, if like
the politicians in Ireland, you take away any preconditions and start
talking, a lot of the obstacles will melt away. Your husband wants to
repair your marriage and that at the moment is enough. Share the
book together. Talk. Slowly, when the pressure is off to explain, he
will begin to open up. He will most probably accept that he has been
a fool (but he won't when he feels attacked). He will probably even
talk about his loneliness while working abroad, his feelings that life
was passing him by and how he got his priorities all wrong (but only
in his own time, not on demand).

So is there hope? Most definitely, start talking, act in good faith
and you will probably not only save your marriage but get all the
answers you need. Demand the answers, before entering into the
talks, and there will be only a huge barrier between you.

Why can't I get over my partner's affair? *You are obsessed
with one element of the affair and can't look past it.*

HOW CAN I COPE WITH MY DISGUST ABOUT MY PARTNER'S EXTREME SEX?

21. How can I ever trust you again? That is my biggest problem. It would be easier if it was a one-time thing or even one person. The guy I married is so good at lying and hiding. We've been together for six years and he has cheated on me for five!! About 12 females have been brought into our marriage. First one was MySpace messages, then a medic he met and was texting like crazy and 'missing her hugs', and each time is far worse, but the last was more than I could imagine.

Eight months ago, we were planning our five-year anniversary cruise and he had me look at his emails to get the account info. I found emails to a hooker and some abbreviations I had to google. He swears he never went and after that was so upset he had to come home. We started marriage counselling and thought it was going so well, but his phone had so much more – there were emails pointing to a long-term affair. It was so ironic because in one message I was being talked about; he told her he had to make a new email account to only write in this one because I was acting bipolar and he had to give me the passwords to his stuff to get me off his back. Along with her there were a lot of other emails to girls online and via contact ads. Stuff I would have never imagined.

He got admitted to psychiatric hospital that night after I confronted him because he claimed he wanted to end it. I called my marriage counsellor and told her he lied again and couldn't continue going. He had to take several weeks off work and while helping him get some stuff from his work locker, I found more evidence of cheating. He didn't want to confess and upset me.

I am ready for my personal appointment at the end of the month. I have told him I am not ready for marriage counselling because there is no trust. Last week I found more junk. He has a translation app, which had the history on more vulgar cheating.

I have hated these last eight months. Part of me wants a divorce. He has ruined me and is so good at lying and letting the world think he's great. He has once again claimed it was the last time and when I asked what makes this one any different he told me he never thought I would leave until this time. Now he is claiming he has found God again.

I don't want my kids to lose their family unity but he has become better at lying and cheating after each affair. He swears he's never touched another female but I want to get tested for sexually transmitted diseases because his emails say he did a lot of stuff. I am searching for a job right now because I've been a stay-at-home mum for five years. I truly don't believe he will ever be faithful. He's even asking since this last time what he has done to make me not trust him. My answer to him was that he's been so good at hiding I never had a clue!

Andrew writes:

I'm afraid infidelity has become worse in the last five years. Smartphones allow more private and explicit interactions. There's more Internet sites to facilitate cheating, Internet porn is full of adverts for prostitutes. It's like throwing petrol onto the fire. So why has your husband been so vulnerable?

Lots of men are so 'nice' and want to 'please their partner', so don't want to rock the boat when they're unhappy. They swallow their pain, they swallow their feelings and they get depressed. Worse still, they use affairs to jolt themselves out of their numbness and feel alive again. In particular, these men want to feel 'connected'. Especially if their wives, in their minds, have become more interested in the kids than them.

However, I wonder if there is something deeper going on with your husband. The volume of women involved, the prostitutes, the extreme sexual practices and the threats to kill himself makes me want to know more about his childhood and whether something extreme happened to him. How would you describe his relationship with his mother and father? Could disciplining him have got out of hand and become abusive? He might even have been sexually assaulted (which has one of two effects when the child grows up – either he or she becomes very withdrawn or cavalier with his or her sexual safety).

The other thing that makes me wonder about your husband's childhood is that he sounds like a small child. 'No I didn't steal the biscuit' (even though I have crumbs round my face and jam on my fingers) has turned into 'I never touched another woman'. How old is he? Seven years old! It's easy to get exasperated but if someone sounds seven it's probably because something traumatic froze a part of him at that point. So despite being a successful businessman, when he's in crisis, he reverts back to a little boy and simply denies everything.

So what do you do? You might decide to try to save this marriage, but I warn you, it's a big mountain to climb. A lot depends on whether your husband is willing to look at why he went off the rails in such a spectacular way – rather than just hide behind finding God. Did he have a proper psychological assessment when he was admitted to hospital? What follow-up do they offer? However, a lot hangs on your reaction too. You could be angry and shame him (and lots of people would say with a solid justification) but this will make him clam up and revert back to the little boy with his hand in the cookie jar. Alternatively, you could be gentle and curious and listen so he begins to open up.

You could work on your relationship, but it means changing yourself too, rather than just lecturing him on his weaknesses. You need to ask yourself – why can't he stand up to me and tell me what he's really thinking? Do you listen to his reasons for being unhappy (even if they make no sense) or do you get angry or tearful and effectively shut him up.

You're faced with a really big decision. Talk to your therapist, take your time and don't rush into anything.

Why can't I get over my partner's affair? *A fresh discovery has sent you back into shock again.*

22. I have been married for almost seven years. My husband's job keeps him away for months at a time. At night he would call to say goodnight and tell me he was exhausted. When the phone log came in he was hanging up on me to call another women and be on the phone for hours. He has been caught 'sexting', sending and receiving porn pictures from girls he has never met. He has cheated many times over. He has been caught masturbating in the bathroom in the middle of the night and has porn downloaded to his phone. The last time he was caught was my birthday. I didn't talk to him – nothing.

After a day or so he came to me and said he thinks he has an issue and looked for an addicts meeting. He went there and then started buying books and joining online therapy groups. He is away now and claims he doesn't leave his room unless it's to work, until he can figure out his triggers and learn control. Does this really sound like an addict? Some of these girls he chatted to and swapped pics with for weeks and months before meeting them for sex. I'm so lost, please help me.

Andrew writes:

It sounds like you've been through a truly horrible time. Catching him looking at porn on your birthday must have really felt like a slap in the face and then there's the cheating too.

Is he a sex and porn addict? This is a difficult question because it is a continuum – a bit like alcohol. It is possible to be a social drinker (with no problems at all) or someone who abuses alcohol (self-medicating, shutting down and coping with difficult or unwelcome emotions) and a full-on addict (where your life is out of control). Sadly, it is very easy for abuse to slip into addiction. The majority of men do use pornography these days as a way of unwinding and as a sexual release. However, they do not use it at inappropriate times (like during your birthday celebrations) or let it tip over into infidelity. So I would definitely think your husband is abusing porn/sex. Ultimately, it does not matter whether he is abusing or an addict. He has a problem that is impacting on your relationship and both of you need help.

The good news is that he is in a treatment programme. Unfortunately, it sounds like it is online, which is better than nothing but does not involve admitting to your problems face-to-face (and dealing with the shame) or getting the full support of other sufferers or a therapist. So I think you need more information about what he's doing and to check whether he's getting enough help.

In addition, you need support too, as this has had a huge impact on you. I would look at joining a group for the partners of love/sex addicts or getting an individual therapist. It will help you understand what's been going on and make you feel less alone (which is really important because this is not the sort of 'news' that you can share with your girlfriends).

Why can't I get over my partner's affair? You're still trying to understand the complexity of your partner's behaviour.

23.

Can I survive in a marriage where my husband wants sex with other women whenever he wants to? I've just flown out to the Far East to join my husband who has been working in Vietnam for two weeks. While he was away, he went to a bar after a tough day and met one of the bar girls in a geisha bar. Soon he was going back every evening, then taking the girl out all Sunday, booking hotel rooms and having sex with her. He describes not wanting the evenings to end and how much fun and laughter they had. This has happened before: Two years ago in transit to Australia he fell headlong for a Thai salon girl (married to an American with a child) and romantic dinners, outings and hotel sex led to his arranging to pay her £400 a month, with a return trip staying in a dream resort all planned until he was prevented by the husband finding out. So instead of flying to join her, he picked up a South African prostitute in the casino of his hotel and took her on a week's road trip. He missed one son's graduation and the second son's twenty-first dinner to do this and tells me he was angry for being cheated of the chance to explore new feelings with the Thai girl and have the break from reality that he desperately needed.

The key to understanding his behaviour is that he hates his job and has to spend long hours doing what he hates. Financial responsibility for his family has, he says, led him to make many lifestyle choices that have boxed him in and emasculated him. He is deeply unhappy and these fantastic encounters in which slim dark-haired pretty girls flirt with him and enjoy his jokes make him feel alive and in touch with his feelings.

His eagerness for sex with them hurts me terribly because through most of the last 15 years of our 23-year marriage he has repulsed all intimacy with me, saying it was too boring to contemplate and gave him nothing. The terrible shock of discovering the Thai girl followed by the South African two years ago, gave us the opportunity to exchange frank feelings and slowly in these two years we have found our way back to increased intimacy and occasional love-making – although not as often as I would like, as I love him and find him attractive. I find the lack of touch, kisses and caresses deeply hurtful and harsh. I am vivacious, slim, pretty and dark haired – all the qualities that he likes. I have desperately tried to share his feelings about his work and to plan a future in which he can chuck it in and shed the load. I have worked all my life and brought up four children with him. It's been the usual juggling and struggling but now we have reached a time in life when we can travel together, do courses together and see an easier future.

But he wants it on his terms. Basically, I am lying here beside him in the dark knowing that last week he was thrilled to be in the arms of a yet another new conquest and that when I tried to make love to him last night, he lay inert because he said I was dull and predictable. He says that it's my problem if I can't accept that it's his right to have other women. He is sorry that it hurts me but it's my problem and if I didn't know it wouldn't hurt.

I've told him that I need cuddles and caresses, that I want to be the one having the dinners and flirting, that it's dangerous to invest in these other relationships as intimacy builds with them and diminishes with me. I had hoped for these golden years to be the best, now that the children need us less and I can retire soon. But I feel that he does not value me enough to be exclusive to me. I feel belittled and confused and very, very weak and stupid. To be honest, if I could die, it would solve his problems, I think. Sometimes, I feel the crushing in my chest like a heart attack. I've lost another stone in weight. I can't sleep and its becoming harder and harder to be the lighthearted, easy companion that he wants. Sometimes I have panic attacks and my windpipe constricts so I can't breathe. I'm holding down my job, my family and trying to keep my husband. He says he doesn't want to leave and that he loves me but does not desire me and that he isn't 'going to service me' in bed. To say that I'm heartbroken doesn't come anywhere near it.

I spend hours poring over self-help books and have read all of yours these past two years; I've been to ten weeks of counselling provided by the sexual health clinic and I've taken a ten-week course in mindfulness. I've bottled up my misery not telling friends and family about the situation, just the counsellor. Only earlier this month he said that he had put 'this silliness' behind him. It is very lonely.

My question is: Can I turn the other cheek and cling on to this marriage to a man that I love, but on these terms?

Andrew writes:

I'm not so much worried about your marriage surviving but the state of your health. Your heart is breaking so much it feels like a heart attack, you can't breathe, you can't sleep and you can't cope. I'm sure everybody reading this letter is going to be screaming out: Leave him! It takes a lot for my mouth to drop open with shock when I read a letter but it did. I kept thinking what a bastard.

However, there are two sides to every story and if you love him, there's got to a good side to him (even though he missed his son's graduation and his other's son's dinner for a date with a hooker!).

So rather than dumping on him – which is very tempting – it would be much better to ask: Why is he behaving so badly? In most cases, it is down to ANGER. He must be incredibly angry with you (and your sons). My guess is that it doesn't come out directly. Despite his bad behaviour, he's probably a really nice guy and if I met him for a drink or at a party we'd probably get along really well. However, the cost of being a nice guy (and everybody liking him) comes at a terrible price. Rather than saying what he needs or standing up for it, he buries the pain and smiles sweetly. Slowly but surely, the pain grows and grows and turns into resentment.

So what could he be angry about? I'm going to take a guess here. As he seems equally angry with his sons, I wonder if he feels that you have consistently put their needs first and his last (and his sexual needs even further down your list). However, he loves his sons and wants the best for them, so he doesn't say anything but swallows his anger – because who wants to admit being jealous of your sons – and you know the rest.

We know that he's angry about doing a job he hates. I'm so pleased that you've told him that he doesn't need to do it (and that you're making strides to make it possible). It's a pity that he didn't tell you he hated it so much that he needed to block out the pain with bar girls. He must be very desperate (or naive) to think this will make him feel better (beyond in the short-term). And he does seem to have a HUGE need to be loved – by everyone – so he doesn't just have sex with these women but romances them, too. Once again, my training asks why?

The most obvious is that he never felt truly loved as a child (beyond when he was a good boy). If you never get unconditional love when you're small, you desperately want it when you grow older. You get married and the fairytale version of love says, 'Everything I do, I do it for you' and at last there's somebody who wants to make you happy. However, married love is more complicated than the movies and songwriters makes us believe. You have children and suddenly you are not only pushed out, but get less sex and have to work even harder.

So can your marriage survive? Let's start with the positives – everything is out in the open. Rather than him swallowing his needs and you taking charge (because someone has to) you can begin to negotiate as two equals. Of course, he can ask: 'Can I sleep around' and you can say, 'No, not on the terms that you're offering' and then you can negotiate. It's called being assertive. However, before any of that can happen, he has to get all this anger off his chest. He needs to tell you all the things that you've done that have contributed to the wall round his heart. It will be horrible – truly horrible but the other alternative is probably worse – carry on as you are!

Why can't I get over my partner's affair? *You need to be assertive rather than alternate between being passive and domineering.*

24. I recently found out that my husband of ten years had an affair with a co-worker. The affair happened three years ago and continued for five months. My husband said it was not just physical and that he felt he loved her and had a connection. The mistress ended the affair since she wanted 'more'. I am really struggling trying to cope with this. I have confronted the mistress and she says it is over. My husband says he loves me and he's truly sorry and wants to stay with me. I am trying to be forgiving... but I know the details of their intimate acts... because I asked for them. They keep playing in my mind like a movie and it is so painful.

I know that he performed oral sex several times on her, but when I'd asked, in the past, he did not perform it on me. For some reason, I am really hung up over this fact and it angers me. I keep asking why he did that to her and not me? He says he doesn't know why. I am associating that intimate act with the fact that he must have loved her more. Can you please provide some insight? Are affairs different and more intimate? How can I move past this? Please help. I'm really struggling.

Andrew writes:

You're right, affairs are different from relationships but not in the way you think. In fact, they are LESS intimate. The problem with sex with someone that you know really well is that it becomes so intimate – you know so much about them – that it becomes harder and harder to experiment. Over time, couples end up having sex with which they feel comfortable but that can easily become a smaller and smaller list carried out in a very similar way. More often that not, it's the same sex you had when you first met – and often that's 20 years ago – and we're not wearing the same clothes, going to the same places and eating the same food!

So why do people do things in affairs they haven't done in their long-term relationships? Firstly, there is no risk. If you give poor oral sex – or whatever – it doesn't matter. You just walk away, and you certainly don't have to deal with a long face at breakfast or be called a pervert for wanting to do something. Secondly, an affair allows people to step outside their normal life and experiment with being someone else. What it doesn't necessarily mean is that he loved her more than you. This is your fear and your personal baggage.

My guess is that you're over-thinking all this, putting two and two together and making three hundred. So let's try and get those horrible images out of your head; I would try three tactics:

1. *Distraction.* (Tell yourself, stop torturing yourself.)

2. *Replace.* (Think about nice things you and your husband have done together.)

3. *Expand your sex life.* (Instead of getting hung up on oral sex – and letting it 'belong' to her – look through some books about sex and find something that appeals that neither of you have done and let that belong to your relationship.)

Finally, allow yourself to be angry. He has cheated on you. You have every right to be angry. My guess is that you've been so keen on getting him back and being forgiving, you haven't allowed yourself to let go of this feeling. Once you have, it will no longer be a barrier between you.

Why can't I get over my partner's affair? *There are issues in your sex life that still need to be addressed.*

25. In *How Can I Ever Trust You Again?* you mention a couple who went through a dark, frantic love-making stage. Our sex life wasn't great before the affair. We have had sex since I discovered my husband had an affair and have noticed it is different. I wrote in my journal that it was 'very physical, almost aggressive and pretty different from what we've done in the past' and when I read about dark, frantic love-making in your book, was relieved to see that it was not uncommon. However, I'd like to hear more about this stage of reconciliation.

Andrew writes:

Having dark, frantic sex after an affair is not unusual and can be really helpful because all the 'safe' rules from beforehand are torn up. At last, you have an opportunity to find a type of love-making that suits who you are today (rather than who you were when you first met and wrote the rules of engagement).

So what's going on? I think there are two different forces at play. The first is to do with the nature of sex (which all too often we try and ignore) and the second is probably something to do with where your relationship is right now.

Let's start with sex. At the very heart of heterosexual sex is penetration, and that involves submission and dominance. In other words, it's all about a power. However, the wonderful thing about mankind is that we have the imagination to challenge this naked truth so it doesn't have to be men in control and women submitting. We play around with positions like woman on top, where in effect she impales herself on her husband's penis and takes control. Couples can experiment with games where she makes him beg to enter her and claims the power for herself. I could go on but I think you get the picture. (However, we often choose to hide the raw power of sex behind romance and a connection of the soul with our beloved, or simply tame it with routine and not making too much noise in case we wake up the kids.) An affair pulls the mask off polite sex and shows us its hidden power, how dangerous it can be and the range of possibilities (if we choose to embrace them).

Sex can also be about ownership – this is MY man or WOMAN. In fact, new lovers often talk about wanting to climb inside each other. However, an affair also makes us realise that we don't OWN our partner and we can't control him or her. Although this is scary it's also a turn-on. Why? Because nobody lusts after what they have, but rather what they don't. Suddenly, you realise how close you came to losing your husband. Having dark frantic sex after an affair allows you to re-connect and possess him again (if only for a few sweaty minutes) and drive out the OW. You are also playing with dominance and submission, in a relatively safe arena, and finding a new balance of power between the two of you.

Let's move on to your relationship. I wonder if the aggression is about anger. Please don't jump to the obvious conclusion: 'He's angry with me for stopping the affair because he loves her more than me.' It could just as easily be about, and most probably is, something far more subtle. For example, he's angry with you for, in his mind, your poor sex life before the affair. He's angry that he had to have an affair before you'd sit up and take notice of his needs. He's angry because you don't listen to his opinions about how to bring up the kids (but always overrule him). He's angry because you're cleverer with words, twists what he says and always win arguments. He might not even be just angry with you but his mother for something (and he's found it hard to express his needs with any woman since). As you can see, I'm just guessing (because I don't know your husband) but there are a million possibilities.

Finally, I would have a discussion about what you've enjoyed about your 'dark' love-making. What could you build on? What would you like to do more often? What else would you like to add to your repertoire to make this is truly a fresh start.

Why can't I get over my partner's affair? *You are trying to fight natural and necessary feelings rather than accepting and learning from them.*

26. I have contacted you in the past about my husband's affair and have read *How Can I Ever Trust You* several times. The good news is that despite failed attempts at counselling etc. your book has really helped both of us and we are now in a really good place. My husband is like the person I first married and we are very happy.

However, despite years of using escort websites on business trips abroad and a six-month affair with a colleague, which was continually denied (culminating in my finding condoms in his bag after a work trip abroad), he has always steadfastly maintained that he has never been sexually unfaithful to me – despite my challenges to the contrary. He does admit to very heavy petting during the affair but nothing else. I just know that this is not the case. Little things, such as items from the minibar in a hotel when he doesn't drink (escort I think); there were only two condoms brought back from the work trip (he says he threw the third one away unused). When I found the condoms and asked him to leave, he rented a flat. Unknown to him, I visited the flat (yes I know, but sometimes people go a bit nuts) and there were candles by the bed. When I visited the flat officially with him to help him pack up, he had new bedlinen and had thrown the other bedlinen away.

So, knowing what I know, and we are in a really good place now, why can't I leave it alone? I ended up on anti-depressants at one point during all this, but am fine and healthy now. I keep asking myself what I would do if I found out the truth and I know it would do us no good at all? I have told him that I do not believe that he has been sexually faith-ful but the time for discussing it has gone and that I do trust him now, and I do. So what do I do to shut my mind off to this?

Andrew writes:

I'm glad that you have found my book helpful for recovering from your husband's affair and although my policy is generally only to answer one letter per person, I thought your question and your approach was really interesting and would help other people.

I liked the idea of telling your husband 'I don't believe you' (espe-cially as his explanations are not very convincing) but, as you point out, the time for cross-questioning his story has passed. What counts now is becoming a team to turn round your marriage.

So how do you get your husband's affair out of your mind? I would suggest three possible strategies:

1. Understand the difference between your feelings and your thoughts (and how the latter influence the former). So next time you're feeling down, stop and name the feeling. I am feeling angry or sad or rejected (or whatever the feeling). You could even say it out loud. The important thing is to witness the feeling – rather than push it away. While I want you to accept your feelings, I suggest challenging your thoughts. Imagine that you're taking dictation and write everything down. Go back over the list and look at the exaggerations – 'never' or 'always' – ask yourself 'What's the evidence for that conclusion?' and check for black-and-white thinking.

2. Try a paradoxical injunction. This involves doing the opposite of what you're trying to achieve. In this case, once a week (or maybe twice) you tell yourself you MUST think about 'my husband's affair' for at least ten minutes – even if you're in a good mood. Drag up all those horrible memories of scouting round the flat and every other hurtful moment; really dig into the pain. Afterwards ask yourself: Was it helpful? Did it move me forwards? The answer will probably be NO. The idea is that you realise firstly that overthinking is not helpful and secondly that you're in control of your mind. You choose to have these thoughts. They are not you.

3. Tackle the feelings about 'my husband's affair' and 'using escort websites' rather than the thoughts? So if you're feeling neglected, ask yourself what would make me feel less neglected? If you're feeling undesired, what would make you feel more desired? Once you've pinpointed something, try asking for something specific. For example, When you're away can we talk every evening on

Skype for half an hour? If you want to feel more sexy and desired, try 'sexting' him or phoning up and reading him a dirty bedtime fantasy (look at Nancy Friday 'My Secret Garden' for some fantasies that turn other women on), or you might even try phone sex.

Once you are not being ambushed by thoughts about his infidelity, you can concentrate on the important issues: improving communication (so if there are issues in the future they are addressed rather than suppressed) and having more fun together (because the couples who have fun together stay together).

Why can't I get over my partner's affair? *You need to understand the link between thoughts and feelings.*

27. My boyfriend of ten years would like to do swinging or have an open relationship. Preferably, he would like to do it with me, but as I don't want to have sex with strangers he thinks I should allow him to do it.

We are definitely soulmates, as we understand each other on many levels. We are similar intellectually but very different socially. He is outgoing, friendly and disorganised, while I am shy, introverted and organised. We complement each other in many respects. We have also learnt a lot from each other in these ten years. I am five years older than him; however, he is more experienced sexually and he helped me become more comfortable with myself in bed. However, I can never imagine myself having sex with someone just for recreational purposes and this is what he would like.

I also must say that I work and earn more than him, I do the housework, etc. He has more time and he only does the DIY (which he actually loves), but I still feel that I work more in and out of the house than him therefore I am more exhausted and have less energy to have sex with him. He has more energy and naturally he has a higher sex drive than me. When I explained that if he helped more I would be less tired and have more energy for him, he got it. However, he did nothing much to change, washing up the plates is the maximum. I also get up way before him. He never notices that I am out the door by 8 am, he gets up around 9, 10 or 11. And that's gone on for the vast majority of the ten years.

I have also agreed over the years to him having time off to work on his hobbies/interests, ie unpaid internship in Brussels, going to university – with my help because he is dyslexic. Now he has gone to Fuengirola, Spain (we live in Madrid) to complete his dive instructor training – he needs to pay some money, which comes out of his inheritance, but living costs come mostly from what I earn and his unpaid work for the dive school. And there in the rented flat he met a woman who became infatuated with him immediately. I was there in the first few days and saw it, so warned him. He brushed it off. Then after I left, they developed a growing fondness for each other, a little kissing, emailing, the woman has taken over what I do for him due to his dyslexia, like organising, cooking, etc! He wants us to live all together, including her young son. He loves her young son. He wants to have one type of sex with me, another with her.

I understand that he has a much higher sex drive than me and much less inhibition than me. He says he loves me deeply, doesn't want to break up with me, but he needs more sex and diverse sex with all sorts of people, ideally living in a commune-style life where everyone loves everyone and he can swing with people he trusts. I can't do this.

So we have been trying to decide if we should break up

because we are who we are and we won't change. I texted him and said that we could have a month break and he can do whatever he does, no questions asked, and then we could try again if I am able to move forward at that point. The idea of losing him seems worse than the idea of him trying out all sorts of women for a month and then coming back to me for the rest of our lives.

I thought this was about my taking responsibility for my shortcomings, but now I am thinking, perhaps I just allow too much for him and justify every one of his shortcomings with 'It's actually my fault'? Is it my fault that I ask him to keep the house clean, not too clean, just to keep it that way after I have cleaned? Is it really a fault that I would like him to work more if he is not career minded? Is it a fault if I get angry and shout when I feel I don't get much physical help? Should I just let him be who he is and not constrain him with my ideas of life? I don't think I have really constrained him, except in that I expected fidelity; that's what I signed up for, after all.

This is the second time something similar happened – or the second time I found out about. It will happen again. Perhaps it's because he was only 23 when we met and couldn't try out his fantasies then – threesomes and other things. But these are not my fantasies and never will be. I don't like strangers touching me, not even a doctor.

In one of your responses to someone else, you mentioned changing boundaries as a child – yes, that was a constant theme in my childhood (and also emotional abuse). I had to take adult responsibilities for my mother's wellbeing and even survival (she had constant suicide attempts, fights with her boyfriends, drinking and the rest of it). I was the adult there, not my mother. So when I met my boyfriend and he needed help with dyslexia I was all too happy to oblige. I think very often I am a sort of mother/carer to him, very often. He was adopted as a baby. His adopted mum was wonderful! She was apparently strict when he was a kid, but by the time I met her, she was so great! I could never have asked for a better mother-in-law, and she has supported me in everything, even when my boyfriend and I had differences in the past. Unfortunately, she passed away a few years ago.

So should I try a trial of one-month open relationship? Could it possibly help – with the proviso that after that, whatever he didn't do he would never try to do – or would it just prolong the inevitable? Sometimes I feel a victim, the next minute I feel the cause of his misery.

Andrew writes:

He wants to live on a commune with swingers and have threesomes and you don't even like being touched by a doctor. I was beginning to wonder why you're even entertaining this idea and thankfully you answered it for me. You were trained – from an early age – to put other people first and cater to their needs. So I want to take a weight off your shoulders: you're not responsible for his misery or his happiness or anything else.

So let's turn to your boyfriend. Why is he so obsessed with fantasy sex? You're going to be surprised at what I'm going to write next, but it's probably got nothing to do with sex at all. After you've picked yourself off the floor, I'll explain. Boys are not encouraged to express their feelings but to suppress them and, obviously, these feelings don't just disappear, they pop up somewhere else. And the place where it's acceptable for men to express their feelings is through sex, so often their emotional problems get located in their penis. So, he could swing with 400 women and an elephant and I still think he would feel empty because he wasn't addressing his core issues, which

I think you've identified as feeling abandoned as a child (by his birth mother).

So if you're still feeling responsible for him, I hope you're beginning to realise that this all started way before you arrived on the scene. However, a 'Miss Fix-it' (like you) would have been very appealing and you'll have recognised the feeling of being needed. (In my trade, this is called the marital fit.) I can understand how you felt like soulmates but you need to ask yourself if this relationship is healthy for you now.

What I hope is that this is going to be turning point for you. You'll read about the impact of having a mother who turned you into her little helper and that will free you of some of the burden you're carrying. At that point, instead of mothering your partners, you'll find an equal. As for your boyfriend, he needs to go on a similar journey, but I fear he thinks he's found his solution: more sex. It's sad that he's going to be trapped in the same old behaviour, but it's not your responsibility – thank goodness. You'll have your hands full with fixing yourself!

Why can't I get over my partner's affair? *It's brought up issues from your childhood that need to be faced.*

WHAT IF HE OR SHE IS STILL IN LOVE WITH THE AFFAIR PARTNER?

28. I've known my wife for over 30 years, our relationship turned romantic 15 years ago and we have been married for 8 years. I discovered that my wife was having an affair about three months ago. She had a previous affair three years earlier but she confessed to that one and we agreed to deal with this without counselling. We have a toddler, who we both love dearly.

We have now attended five relationship therapy sessions. She has not been able to say anything about the affair until the last session, when she admitted when the affair started (about one year or so) and nothing about why or what the other person gave her that is lacking in our relationship (we both agree that communication is part of the problem). Although she has confirmed at every session that she does want to give our relationship another go, three months after stopping contact with her lover she continues to have surprisingly strong feelings for him and her love for me is not returning.

I've found the last three months very difficult and emotionally draining and wondered whether it's possible to really make any progress on our relationship when she obviously is still in love with someone else? She says that if she could she would 'flick a switch' to make things better. My questions are:

1. What can I do, what can she do (or not, as the case may be) to help make progress on the ILYB issue?

2. How long will it typically take for her to move on from her lover?

3. How long could it take for her love for me to return?

Andrew writes:

I am pleased that you have started counselling but concerned that so little has been discussed about the adultery. Before I answer your questions, I have one of my own for you to consider. Why has it taken so long for your wife to give even the barest information about her affair?

My guess is that it's a combination of several things... firstly, she feels guilty and the affair will not present her in the best light (I call these selfish motives). My second guess is that she is frightened of hurting you (I call these altruistic motives). There is little that you can do about the first but you can do something about the second. If she tells you the truth, are you likely to collapse into a heap of tears and emotions? If so, you are inhibiting her honesty and without honesty it is impossible to move forward. So you will need to harden your heart and listen quietly, unresponsively and keep your wits about you – so that you can ask relevant questions. Afterwards you can break down.

So here are my thoughts on your questions:

1. *What can you do to make progress?* Insist on her telling the story of the affair. Until she brings it out into the real world, the affair remains a secret carefully preserved in its own romantic little bubble. Talking about the details – like what she did for childcare while she was having sex with her lover – will make her realise just how sordid, deceitful and unpleasant her behaviour has been. You need to hear about his circumstances – my guess is that he was equally two timing and his behaviour equally squalid. He is not the romantic paragon that he is able to remain while your wife hides behind secrecy. Hearing the details will make you decide if you still want to be with a woman who has cheated not once but twice. If she is forgiven too easily, she'll not feel that she has deserved it and, to be honest, I doubt she will respect you.

2. *How long for her to move on from a lover?* You are worried about whether she will love you again but the real question should be whether you can trust her again! However, answering your question... if someone is prepared to cut contact and not feed the dying flames, I would hope that they would feel significantly different in six months time.

3. *How long would it take for her love to return for you?* Her love for you cannot return until the affair is resolved. As you discovered after the first affair, just pretending that everything has returned to normal solves nothing. However, the good news is an affair brings all the problems – what I call the dead bodies in the relationship – floating up to the surface where they can finally be sorted. So there is a real opportunity here. However, you will have to be brave, use the support of your counsellor and push for the truth. It will be tough but if you were my clients, I would expect to see you for probably five months or so and by the end, I would be crossing my fingers that bursting the affair bubble, better communication, and working through the underlying problems that caused the affairs will provide the foundation for love returning.

Finally, I want to make a general comment about women who cheat on their husbands – not once but twice. I've counselled several women in this situation – sometimes on their own and sometimes with their partners. However, I hear a different story from the women on their own because the others are frightened to tell the truth for fear of destroying their men's ego. So let me spell it out. Women like strong men. They want to feel safe and protected from the world. They want a lover not a friend – they have millions of women friends and don't need another one. (I'm interested that you were friends for 15 years before your relationship turned romantic.) I bet you're a nice guy, a really nice guy who always put her first. When you're angry with her behaviour, you swallow it up – read the other letters from other guys and you'll see yours is cool, detached and although full of pain, completely devoid of passion. Obviously, I don't want you to be someone who you're not but I want you to stand tall.

So this is what you can do. Insist on hearing the full details without rushing to make everything better (like a friend might, but be angry about being betrayed like a lover). I know I've made this point about three times in my reply but it's because I fear you'll cave in too soon. When something upsets you, tell her about it like an equal partner (rather than as a friend who could swallow the upset because she or he doesn't have to live with her 24/7). Take charge in the bedroom rather than just catering to her needs. Become selfish and think about what you need and like sexually (rather than 'I'll do anything you want'). Let yourself go, enjoy sex and the passion will come through. In this way, you will become her equal rather than a courtier.

Why can't I get over my partner's affair? *You have been so focused on your partner that you have neglected your own needs.*

29. Four months ago, I discovered that my husband of 19 years had been having an affair for the past year. I was willing to 'forgive' and set about the business of rebuilding/re-creating our marriage and on 'discovery day' this is what he said he wanted too.

Unfortunately, he has changed his mind five times since. This has included him coldly telling our teenage children that he'd been having an affair and was going (on two separate occasions) and conversely that he'd decided to stay. He also moved out of the family home for four weeks to live with his mistress but then decided his life was with me. Again, I willingly and optimistically agreed to rebuild our marriage.

We have been back together for nearly five weeks now and for the majority of the time things are very good. We are communicating well; we go out and do fun things together and as a family, and we have spiced up our sex life. He is in the process of winding down the new home that they set up together but every time he goes to the house I feel vulnerable and uncertain as to whether he's going to change his mind again. He admitted that he wouldn't be disappointed if she was there and that he couldn't 'just switch off his feelings for her'. Ouch.

What is the best way for me to handle these feelings that he still has for 'her'? I know he has 'chosen' me so would I be best to just let his feelings for her remain private? Should I stop asking questions which ultimately allude to answers that I don't want to hear – although I accept that feelings don't come with an off switch, I don't want to hear it from him.

I feel so vulnerable that he's going to change his mind again. I believe that we can have a brilliant future together so I'm consciously not allowing my fear to direct me to do something I know I'll regret, ie ask him to leave, thus pre-empting any decision-making on his behalf that I accept I could well be imagining. Additionally, I couldn't be the source of any further mental trauma for the children – I feel that I would happily settle to protect their mental well-being.

I guess I'd really appreciate some advice regarding how long his feelings of 'love' for her are likely to last once their shared rental home has been wound up. I'd also appreciate guidance on how to handle my feelings of pain as he does still have feelings for her. If you could throw in a pearl of wisdom on how to conquer vulnerability that would be brilliant!

Andrew writes:

I think we might be coming from different places on this one. You seem to want to control your feelings – you ask twice about 'handling' emotions – so you can subdue the pain and conquer your vulnerability. When your husband can't 'switch off his feelings', you go 'ouch'. As if that's exactly what you hoped he'd done when he came back. You accept that feelings 'don't come with a switch' but deep in your heart, you think it might be a good idea! Finally, you are prepared to 'settle' if this protected your children – which I think means only having half your husband's heart as long as he is physically present.

However, I want you to ACCEPT your feelings. They are clues about how to behave rather than spanners that stop your well-oiled world from working. So you're hurt, anxious and sometimes frightened. I know those are horrible feelings but they are worse still if you tell yourself you shouldn't feel them. In most cases, there is probably a good reason for you to feel vulnerable. Discuss it with your husband and perhaps together you can find a way round it. If you're frightened, I bet it's because there are issues that need to be dealt with. Fear is a clue to look deeper not something that needs to be squashed down.

So here's my pearl of wisdom that you asked for: *If you conquer vulnerability, you shut out love.* We don't love invulnerable things. We love puppy dogs and kittens not tanks (beyond a subset of men on the autism scale). I'm going to throw in another pearl for free. If you understand the complexity of your own feelings – both positive and negative – you will have a little more tolerance for your husband when he comes up with shades of grey on the journey ahead (rather than the black and white you'd prefer).

So how long will the 'feelings' last? My hope is that your husband's feelings have already fallen off the cliff (where lust, secrecy and bubble world pumps up everything to massive proportions). However, I would not be concerned if he finds himself 'thinking' about her from time to time. Looking back at the relationship and reviewing what happened (and wondering how much was fantasy and how much reality) is all part of the healing process. In effect, he needs to mourn before he can let it go. My hope would be that slowly over the next three months, she will slowly drop out of his thoughts (and then days will pass by without thinking about her). Six months will be a major landmark and he could even begin to doubt that he ever really loved her.

However, I want to put a warning in big letters. So here goes: IT IS UNLIKELY EVERYTHING WILL GO IN TEXTBOOK FASHION. In the real world, ex-lovers are weak. They have an argument with their partner, they're feeling down and look at their ex's Facebook page. Their partner finds out and there's another row. It's not because their 'love' for the ex is so strong or because their relationship with their partner is not strong enough. It's because human beings are fallible. In textbook 'end of affair' scenarios, the other woman or man drops off the radar and are not considered. However, they are flesh and blood too. They get a bit tipsy and send begging texts or try and make their ex-lover feel guilty. The temptation to reply is huge and once again, these texts will be discovered and there's another round of pain. So trust me, everything will not go straightforwardly. It might take a longer or shorter time. In the greater scheme of things, it doesn't matter – just that you can cope today, tomorrow and the day after. Pretty soon, you're out the other side.

My other fear is that it will take YOU a lot longer to forget her. In this way, the danger is more to do with how you react – rather than what's going on his head. If he can report contact – for example, over winding up the flat or random emails from her – without getting an explosion of tears or accusations, you might be able to deal with this as a team (rather than him going back to keeping secrets, or more accurately, being economical with the truth).

Whenever, you're feeling down, try channelling your energy into learning about yourself and why your marriage was vulnerable – rather than obsessing about her – and you'll transform this experience from something dangerous into an asset for your relationship.

Why can't I get over my partner's affair? *You need to focus more on getting through today rather than worrying about an unknowable future.*

30. I have been together with my partner for six years and we have a five-year-old and a nine-month old baby. My partner had an affair a year ago (when I was pregnant), which was apparently just one night, but since then it has been developing into what he says is a genuine relationship – but entirely through the Internet.

He only told me the truth five months ago, and we have all been through some very, very dark times. My partner is completely devastated by what he has done, and it has turned into a deep existential crisis, with him questioning past decisions, his relationship with his family, his hopes, dreams and aspirations about the future, etc. Even though he won't acknowledge it, I am fairly convinced that he is showing many symptoms of depression too.

The main problem is that he cannot decide between me and her. He says he can't let her go, but he also can't let me go. He says he loves both of us in equal measure (which I still find incredible considering the geographical distance in his relationship with her... but it was all sparks and deep connection apparently, so I try not to question that any more).

I am feeling much stronger in myself than a few months ago, but I still go through phases of wanting to throw in the towel; phases of wanting to stick by him to help him through his crisis; optimistic phases of thinking that if I sit it out and wait and believe in the fact that it will work out for us it will; and phases of just waiting to see what happens.

I have just finished reading *How Can I Ever Trust You Again?*, and it's somewhat upsetting because the book is mostly written for couples with whom the affair has ended, but for me, it still hasn't. She is still there... waiting for him. And he is driving himself completely crazy trying to decide, decide, decide. But, so far, he can't decide. It's been a year now since this happened to him. How much longer can I really wait?

Andrew writes:

What a horrible situation, for you, your husband and your children. One thing is certain... none of you can carry on like this for much longer. So what needs to be done?

First, please show this reply to your husband – as I hope it will prompt a different kind of conversation from the ones you've had before (ie: should I stay or go, who do I love the most? Why can't you give her up? etc).

Let's start with why your husband went off the rails in the first place. When men cheat during their partner's pregnancy, it is a clear signal that they are uncomfortable about becoming a father. Sometimes it triggers a crisis about their own father (as they are frightened of becoming like him) or 'How on earth am I going to support all these people?' – especially if you hate your job and dream of doing something else (because now you're trapped forever). Or with a second child, it's a fear that it will be like the first time (but pushed further down the list of your wife's priorities) and you'll never be given sex again (because sex is the one way that it is socially acceptable for men to let down their barriers and get close to someone). Finally, if a man says, 'I wasn't that keen on having a baby' and basically 'I did it for you' or (in some cases) 'I felt tricked into it', their wives pour a bucket of scorn on them and accuse them of not loving their daughter or son or being a monster (possibly because she's got her own dark second thoughts and needs to clamp down on them too). So it becomes an off-limits topic or shut down with the words: 'Our baby is here now so shut up and get on with it!'

Guess what... if you're trying to cope with all those feelings – and men have nowhere to take this stuff – talking to another woman on the Internet or, even better, forgetting your troubles with a quick shag seems very attractive. Stupid though, because it makes everything worse. Your wife finds out, you feel like a heel, but nothing gets sorted. You feel so much shame that you'll do anything to feel better, and guess what, she's still waiting at the end of a click. But once, again it's the wrong solution... because everything is now a million times worse.

Now let me get on to Internet affairs... they are based on a fantasy of someone knowing us and 'deep' connections. However, we don't really know this person or how they are in everyday life. We're not our real selves either. There's no responsibilities. We can be whoever we want to be and they can be whoever we want them to be (because there's no inconvenient reality getting in the way).

In an ideal world, you would both go into therapy together and talk through all your real issues (rather than this affair which is really the tip of the iceberg). He would cut all contact with this OW – and follow my programme for shutting off feelings for the affair partner. When he felt down and alone, he would take his feelings to you – rather than go back online and spark off the whole saga – and you'd be caring and understanding about his down days (even if you felt angry and upset that he was still thinking about the OW). Sadly, we live in the real world and that's far more complicated.

However, if he really can't give up this woman (and really mean it, rather than mean it for five minutes and slip – like an alcoholic who can't give up drink), there is often only one way to break the dead lock. The OW is caught up in the fantasy – normally because her life is a mess and she needs someone to save her – so she won't break it off. Your husband is too worried about hurting other people to make a decision. So I'm afraid you will have to make the decision. I know this is not fair but I say it for two reasons. Firstly, you can't go on like this for much longer. Secondly, he could realise within about two months that about 50 per cent of their 'deep connection' is in his head. In the cold light of day, the bubble will burst and he might be finally ready to do the work.

The big danger is he will 'blame' you for 'ending' the relationship – or you will blame yourself if he goes and does not return – so you have to be really sure. When you're about to reach the end of your patience, and truly mean it, explain the situation to your husband. Discuss what a trial separation might look like, issues about contact with the children, bank accounts, etc. In this way, it is more of a mutual decision and you're far less likely to regret it than simply snapping one day and asking him to leave.

Why can't I get over my partner's affair? *You need to build yourself up and feel strong enough to decide your next move.*

31. My wife is in love with a woman. I'm convinced she's just bi and not fully a lesbian, but her heart and body is with the OW right now. She kept her affair a secret for a year when I found out by chance. I think she has feelings for me and our five-year-old son. So I instinctively opened up communication between us and felt closer to her than ever before. But she won't let me show any affection with her, saying she loves her girlfriend and wants to see her as soon as she can.

Right now I'm getting the impression it's turning into a weird yo-yo affair where she sees me for a lot of things that she needs and her for love and sex. I admit I dropped the ball when it came to loving her after our son was born, which is partly why things are like this. I get the impression that she realises her affair will likely fail and is toying with my feelings to keep me as a back-up option. We've been married for eight years and I'm not sure what I should do.

Andrew writes:

Let's start with the good news: I don't think she is either toying with your feelings or using you as a back-up option. I expect she is completely torn. On one hand, she cares deeply for you (and will not want to hurt you) plus she wants to keep the family together for the sake of your son. However, on the other hand, she has discovered a whole new side to her sexuality and fallen in love with another woman. Although it feels terribly personal, it is more about her than you (so please don't beat yourself up).

Like you say, this affair is probably not going to last (as most don't) and I expect her girlfriend is putting a lot of pressure on her to come out. However, sexuality is a complex matter and everybody has to discover themselves at their own pace (rather to appease someone else). I think this combination, plus the yo-yo nature of their relationship, will make the future of this affair very uncertain. In addition, you might be right that your wife has fallen for this *particular* woman and might not feel the need or urge to have a relationship with any OW. However, I'm less certain of this.

Let me try and put you in your wife's shoes for a moment. When she was growing up there would have been far less information about being lesbian and the few characters on soap operas and the like would probably have seemed exotic and strange. With lots of pressure to conform, it's perfectly possible for lesbianism to never have crossed your wife's mind or to be something that other people did (or she could have simply buried her feelings). It is not unusual for women to discover this side of their sexuality when they're older, under less pressure to belong to a gang and know themselves better.

Whatever the situation for your wife, she will be feeling a strange sense of exhilaration (because she has stopped hiding), shame (because there are still a lot of negative images about lesbianism and for hurting you) and fear (about the future). These are extremely strong emotions and she'll be tossed and turned first one way and then the other. Please be compassionate and patient (because it will take her a while to work out what she wants).

You might be surprised to discover that this situation is quite common. Crispin Blunt is a Conservative MP who came out as gay and had to fight his local constituency party to avoid being deselected. When asked his wife's reaction, he said: 'One of Victoria's complaints in the marriage was that she could never reach me inside, that there was always a protected part of me, which, of course, there was. Now our relationship is actually much more relaxed. I'm her gay best friend. We have lovely conversations. We are open with each other, united around our children.' So think, have you felt shut out from your wife? How has that made you feel about yourself?

So what should you do? The Straight Spouse Network supports the spouses of people whose partners become gay, lesbian or bi-sexual. They report that one-third of marriages break up right away, one-third after trying to save the marriage (because the partner truly is gay or lesbian) and a third stay together and the gay / lesbian partner has sexual partners on the side. You have to ask yourself, if she does want to return to the marriage whether you will feel safe, secure and truly wanted (rather than going through the motions)? Although you're thinking of your marriage and your son, you have to consider that you need love, affection and to be desired, too.

Why can't I get over my partner's affair? *You need to give your partner time and space to sort through her feelings rather than expect her to fit into your timetable for moving forward.*

HOW CAN I COPE WHEN MY PARTNER CHEATED AND HAD A CHILD?

32. My husband's mistress had a baby four months ago and I am struggling to cope with this as well as the knowledge that the affair had been going on for ten years. We are trying to stay together but I don't know how to cope with there being a baby. He sees her once a week but the affair is over (so he says). I am trying not to nag but I feel very angry a lot of the time and want to say nasty things to punish him, and there always seems to be an atmosphere at the weekend when the visit is due. I don't know what to do to try and cope with the situation and move forward – help!

Andrew writes:

When I did my training, the advice we were given for dealing with a child being born from an affair was straightforward. The husband should either have no contact (just the basic legal and financial commitments) or the wife is fully involved and the baby is integrated into the family (just like a child from a previous marriage).

Unfortunately, they didn't tell us that both options are incredibly difficult and fraught with pitfalls. Fortunately, I've counselled several couples in this position. I can explain the pluses and negatives of each option, and if you know what's likely to go wrong, you won't feel such a failure when there are setbacks – forewarned is always forearmed.

No contact

At first sight, this looks perfect. There's a clean break and that's got to be best for your marriage. It's also concrete proof that you're his number one priority. However, there are five key pitfalls:

1. **Your husband will be full of shame and guilt for 'letting down his baby' and this will be played on by the mistress.** I know he should also be feeling shame and guilt for letting you down but, in his mind, by staying with you he's doing the right thing.

2. **Your husband wants to save your marriage and will agree to anything.** At the time, he will say 'no contact' and mean it but he's got all this guilt and shame and now he's had time to reflect he's wondering if the second option would be better. He doesn't dare to say anything in case there's more tears and anger, so that brings me to point three.

3. **Your husband is likely to lie.** This is not because he's a bad man but because lying is the only way to keep two people happy (his mistress and you) and he's spent years doing just that. He's in the habit of solving an immediate crisis by promising the moon and stars (to both of you), but that just puts off the evil moment until you discover the secret texts, a new email account, start following her on Twitter, etc, etc.

4. **Your husband needs to mourn.** Perhaps he's already met the baby and bonded or perhaps he needs to mourn the idea of being involved in the baby's life. Unfortunately, mourning involves a lot of thinking about the baby and many men mistake that for a sign that he 'should' be involved with the child. In a weak moment, it's easy to assuage the guilt by sending a text to enquire about the baby's health (and not feel such a monster – at least until you find out about it).

5. **You will get angry and threaten to end the relationship.** A couple of days later, you will feel sorry and take back everything – you were tired or it was in the aftermath of finding another text. Unfortunately, it reinforces his doubts about whether it's possible to save the marriage and encourages him to keep his options open (and check out her Facebook page).

Integrated into the family

This option has compassion for the child, who is 'innocent', and if you're truly involved – and seeing all the emails, etc – you know he's not going behind your back and you can begin to rebuild trust. However, there are five key pitfalls:

1. **His mistress had a baby to 'win' your husband.** In her mind, full of magical thinking, if he holds his baby in his hands often enough the 'scales will fall from his eyes' and he will 'know' that he should be with her. In other words, she's not just looking for a father for her child but a husband too. She is unlikely to 'play nice'.

2. **He can't have a relationship with the baby without a relationship with the mother.** With an older child, you can phone them and check when you should pick them up at the weekend (and they can ask their mum if that suits). With a small baby, access will always involve seeing the mother and she is extremely unlikely to pass the baby over to the father and let him take it out of her sight. She is even less likely to let his wife be part of this access – because mistresses see the wife as a witch (or how can else can they seek to destroy her marriage?).

3. **The mistress needs to be mature and put the interests of the baby first.** I would like to think this is going to happen but true adults don't put all their faith in magical thinking. It's also easy for her to imagine the best interests of the baby to be the same as her best interests. So the mistress tells herself it would be best for her baby to have a full-time father (because that's what she wants), helping you save your marriage by cooperating over access is highly unlikely.

4. **Your husband is still going to lie.** He wants to keep everybody sweet so he will tell white lies – like he's only going to call into the

first birthday party for half an hour – when he has already agreed to help clear up afterwards.

5. **Everybody needs to be a great communicator to make it work.** Sadly, your husband is a people pleaser (and says what will keep other people happy). That's why he didn't speak up about his unhappiness, or say that he didn't agree about something (to keep the peace) and end up being so low that he was tempted by an affair. You're angry, hurt and resentful and that doesn't make for good communication either. Finally, the mistress probably has an unspoken agenda and will say one thing but do another.

Finally, I wouldn't be surprised if you're full of despair. But it is possible to find a way forward – if only slowly and with lots of good communication. Here are my five best tips from the coal face of trying to work this in the real world:

1. **It is natural to get angry.** So please don't beat yourself up if your good intentions slip. It's fine to report your anger – 'I'm angry with you because...' but not to say 'nasty things to punish him', or generally take it out on your husband. I know I'm asking a lot, but that's why you need to seek personal counselling to help you recover from the shock and mourn the loss of the 'great' husband that you thought you had and accept the 'doing his best under difficult circumstances' husband.

2. **Don't indulge in magical thinking.** It's easy to think, 'If he stops contacting her' everything will be fine or to believe 'If he truly loved me, he wouldn't....' In reality, he might be slowly but surely giving up on contacting her or means to stop lying (but kept back information until what he hoped would be a 'better time'), but it takes time to break bad habits. In addition, it is possible to love you and want to know how the baby is doing. I would also counsel

against the magical thinking that 'divorce will make me feel better.' Of course divorce is an option – and one some people choose – but don't expect it to make everything better. Your husband will still be torn between two families and all the poor communication and lies will still be there (but you'll have less influence over him). You'll also still be angry but for different reasons.

3. **Don't set arbitrary tests.** The most common one is 'any contact behind my back and that's the end'. However, contact does not have to be a setback. I was counselling a couple where he did meet up with the mistress for a drink. His wife was initially angry, of course, but she kept calm and discovered that she felt more resigned than anything. It helped that he told her about it (although a few weeks afterwards). Under these circumstances, they were able to talk properly (because he didn't get defensive) and see the situation for what it really was, a set back rather than the end of the world. Ultimately, the drink made the man have a clearer perspective on his ex-mistress and start to think, 'What did I see about her in the first place?'

4. **Break the future into manageable chunks.** If you focus on getting through the next few months, this situation seems possible. If you start thinking about forever, that's when it gets too much and you'll both start to catastrophise. In addition, there will probably need to be different solutions when the child is different ages. The mistress will probably have given up her fantasy of a full-time father (and might marry someone else) and you will feel differently too. So any solution, at this point, is going to be a temporary one.

5. **Keep talking.** Although it seems like you're staring into a black abyss, if you keep talking you will find chinks of light. It helps if you don't let every argument become about the baby, especially if it's really about leaving the top off the orange juice and it spilling

all over the kitchen floor. In addition, talking (and listening) will help you improve your communication skills and that's an asset whatever happens.

I hope this helps and wish you all the best.

Why can't I get over my partner's affair? *You have been really hurt and it will take time to recover.*

33. I have been with my husband for a long time and I found out five years ago that he had an affair with a work colleague. She had a baby from this relationship. Initially my husband wanted both of us to show 'a united front' and go to the hospital after the child was born. I refused and said that I could not cope with seeing the third party and the child: a constant reminder of the betrayal. At that point I said that he could have contact with the child but we would have to part. He made the decision to stay.

I am writing because it is over five years ago since the affair and although he says he has not had any contact, I still feel betrayed, hurt and cannot believe that he could do this to us. He said his thoughts were always with me, but this does not make me feel better, only worse. Obviously thoughts of me were not enough for him to stop the affair.

I still love my husband and he loves me; however, I cannot live with the knowledge of the affair and the child. I feel at this point that a divorce would be the best way forward, as I would be able to draw a line under our marriage and move on. Can you give me any advice? Your book talks about things improving after six months and this has been five years. What can I do, why can't I accept what has happened and move on?

Andrew writes:

Let's start with the positives: you love your husband and he loves you. This is definitely a foundation for saving your marriage.

However, whenever there is a baby born from an affair, it makes recovery much harder. While a relationship that ended five years ago is in the past and something abstract, a five-year-old child is running around, very real and very much in the present. There are also a million and one worries about what will happen in the future and whether he or she will knock on your door.

Reading your letter, it seems that the two of you have become stuck somewhere along the recovery process and if you ever try and talk about it, you immediately fall into the same old rut:

Husband: 'But my thoughts were always with you.'

You: 'Not enough to stop you!'

Husband: Silence.

You: *(Thinks)* Game set and match to me.

Husband: *(Feels)* Less likely to open up and more resentful and distant.

You: *(Feels)* More hurt and betrayed.

So how can you break the loop? If you really wanted a divorce you would be consulting a solicitor rather than writing to me. From reading your letter, I'm not certain exactly what you feel hurt and betrayed about? Probably you're having trouble pin-pointing it too because on the face of it, he's been doing everything right. He's stopped the affair. He says he's not in contact with his ex-wife. He's complied with your wishes for no contact with the child. You say he loves you and you love him.

I keep thinking of the night before I moved into my current house – over 25 years ago. I couldn't sleep and kept tossing, worried that I'd bought pale carpets, which would 'show every mark' and had cost a lot of money. In the cool light of day, I could see that my worries were not about the carpets. I had lots of other fears: it was a large house, costing what at the time seemed like a huge sum of money and there were was a chain that could have broken at any point. However, somehow all these shapeless and nameless concerns had alighted on something concrete: cream carpets. Once I'd realised what was happening, I could break my anxiety down into the constituent parts, deal with the bits that I did have control over and let go of the bits that I didn't. I wonder if the child has become the repository of all your fears: some about your husband, some about the affair, some about your relationship and some about yourself (and the unsettling things you've learnt about yourself over the past five years).

I wonder if you made a list of all the things that need to change in your marriage, what would be on that list? So, for the time being, I want you to put the child to one side and calmly tell your husband about your unhappiness, tell him you're considering divorce and sharing what you think needs to change. Ask him for his 'to be fixed' list. Spend time together discussing whether you want to try again or whether it is too painful. It could be when you take the child out of every argument – either spoken or unspoken – you will be able to find a way forward, he will make you feel cherished enough to forgive and your marriage will survive.

Why can't I get over my partner's affair? *You keep going round and round the same loop.*

WOULD I FEEL BETTER IF I HAD REVENGE?

34. I found out about four months ago that my husband had been seeing someone for a five- or six-week duration. We have been married for 20 years and have three children. It has absolutely devastated me. I have taken responsibility for his need to feel wanted but not for the choice he made in meeting up with this woman once a week for sex. By all accounts she seduced him and he went for it. She is married and has two children. I discovered the affair after he accidentally sent a text to our daughter. He therefore had to explain to all of us. It was horrendous. He is completely remorseful and knows he has made the biggest mistake of his life. He immediately told this to the woman and has had no contact with her since. She lives in our village but our paths do not cross. I know how bad he feels and he has been so desperate, he has felt suicidal. I have feared for him but at the same time I cannot hold back my hurt and anger for fear of what he might do. He has been trying to make it up to me and our children ever since and I know he wants more than anything to fix this mess. My eldest daughter hit the nail on the head when she said immediately that this was completely out of character for him.

We have always had something very special but had lost our way in recent years after our middle daughter died. She was severely disabled, so our lives have never been easy and we never really had any help, practically or emotionally. We have almost lived separate lives but underneath all of that, neither of us has ever wanted anyone else and the basic foundations of our marriage have been solid. We were rarely intimate and took to doing things on our own.

However, we made changes immediately and in this short space of time rekindled the deep love we have always had and it feels completely right and so good at times. We are on the right road together and I'm trying so hard to look forward. I do, however, still visualise them together. I am still so angry that he deceived me and still just so angry and hurt that I'm still completely broken. I love my husband so much and I know he does me. He always has and he has only ever wanted me. I know that. I know this was a cry for help and I'm trying to be positive about things; I know this could be the making of us. However, I have this need for revenge.

I don't hate my husband although I hate what he has done, but I could kill this woman with my bare hands. I confronted her after two months. She had no idea who I was. I told her in a very calm manner that there was a lot I could say to her but just to remember that I could bring her family down in seconds. She looked shell-shocked and said nothing. I got back in my car and calmly drove off.

One of the problems is that I feel she has got away with it. Her family know nothing. My family has been torn apart. My daughters have been distraught and obviously question their father now over everything and live in fear that we will not get through this. My eldest daughter is 18, and while she loves him, she questions him and his moves like a suspicious wife. I am absolutely livid that this woman seduced my husband and has damaged my family. I know my husband well enough to know that while he obviously went along with it, his reasons would have been completely different to hers. He has not had it easy and I'm certainly no pushover, but as I said earlier I have taken part responsibility for some of this. Where do I go from here? I have days when I can put it to one side in my head but others are filled with so much raw emotion that I feel I'm not in control of my thoughts and possibly not my actions.

Andrew writes:

I'm going to deal with the question of revenge in the second half of this letter, but first I want to acknowledge how difficult everything has been over the past two years. Bereavement is something that is incredibly difficult to cope with and overcome. People do do some incredibly crazy things to feel better and, as your husband has found, just end up piling pain on top of pain.

However, there's a bit in your letter that really concerns me. On one level I've got no problem with the fact that you're very angry and that's a perfectly natural human reaction. What I'm particularly worried about is that you feel 'not being in control of your thoughts and possibly not my actions'.

As you're discovering, our actions are often linked to our thoughts and although I'm not certain that you need to 'control' your thoughts (or whether it's possible) you *have* to be responsible for your actions. (Otherwise you're in the morally dubious position where you're claiming 'you made me do it'.) So let's start with examining thoughts; they can rise unbidden – whether you like it or not. For example, I've had a client whose partner had been unfaithful during a business trip to China and every time the country came on the news – even about something unconnected like an earthquake or pollution levels in Beijing – she would feel her stomach lurch and she'd be reminded of his infidelity. Of course, she cannot control these associations. However, she can choose what happens next. She can decide to let this developing thought go or she could seize on it, turn it over in her mind, throw in lots of other thoughts about the affair, start to ruminate, and finally, obsess about it.

We have hundreds, maybe thousands of thoughts a day and another one will be along in a moment. Most probably a fairly benign one – like 'What are we going to have for tea?' So I would suggest labelling the thoughts – 'Oh there's another association with the affair'. This will help you distance yourself enough to make a choice: Do I want to stop and examine that thought or shall I let it float past? If you decide to unpack the thought, be aware of the type of thinking. It is helpful – because it is allowing you to make sense of what happened? Is it grieving – either for your daughter or the years of your marriage wasted through living separate lives? Is it ruminating – which is unhelpful – because it ties together disparate parts of your life that might not belong together and makes everything seem even bleaker? Is it catastrophising – which involves exaggerated thinking and claims that you'll 'never' get over these problems and your life will be 'forever' tainted'? What you will discover is ruminating and catastrophising is what leads to thoughts about revenge.

While you can't stop developing thoughts or avoid your equivalents of 'China', you can control what you do next. You can label your thought: 'That's a trigger' or 'That's a developing thought' and simply focus on the next item on the news, or you can switch channels when, for example, the characters in a soap opera are having an affair. Alternatively, you might need a good 'wallow' and decide to give yourself a chance to grieve.

Let's move on to the second part of my answer and your fear that the OW has 'got away with it'. Ultimately, all stories – and your letter is a story too – have three possible endings. They are revenge, tragedy and forgiveness and there are simply no other options. Now the problem with revenge is that you never quite know what's going to happen. If you blow apart her marriage, who knows, she might try and exact revenge on you and your marriage sinks down to a further level of hell. Will it really make you feel better in the cold light of day? I think it's going to make you feel dirty and not like yourself very much. It's probably going to terrify your husband and set back your recovery. He might even question if he can love someone whose heart is consumed with vengeance. That's one of the reasons why revenge sometimes tips into the second ending: tragedy.

I know forgiveness is incredibly hard and it's probably far too early to forgive your husband and certainly the OW (and ultimately, you may decide that you don't want to forgive her). But you do need to be able to forgive yourself (for being distracted and not as aware of your husband's issues as you might have been) and, at some point, your husband (for not speaking up about the problems), or your story will not have a happy ending.

Why can't I get over my partner's affair? *Looking for revenge keeps you bound to the past and stops you making a better future.*

35. Please can you help me? I have recently discovered (a month ago) my husband had a two-month affair with a work colleague. To say I was devastated is putting it mildly. However, I have decided to forgive him, and we are working hard on recovering and have taken so much from your book *How Can I Ever Trust You Again?*.

My problem is the severe anxiety I have over the OW. I confronted her when I found out. I went into the workplace and spoke my mind; verbally abused her by calling her ugly, fat, etc. She is now threatening to come into my workplace and humiliate ME. My husband is still working with her and she keeps commenting to him that she is furious at how he has used her and how I have abused her. I am so fearful she is going to do something to get her revenge. My husband is looking for another job but it's not easy. I am sick to the stomach most of the time, can't sleep or eat. I am taking anti-depressants but they do not help with the anxiety.

I feel so strongly that I need to be prepared in case this OW does 'attack' me. I feel threatened because I know she can emotionally wound me. My husband agrees the threat is real and that she may well confront me – and so he did confess other misdemeanours he hadn't previously disclosed in case she informed me of events I didn't know about. I was heart-broken to hear that there was more than I initially thought, but we are working it out. I am determined to mend my marriage as I love my husband very much. He made a stupid mistake. I accept that. He didn't care for this woman at all.

Please can you help? I'm feeling desperate.

Andrew writes:

First of all, you need to remind yourself that you've had a horrible shock. Your husband has had an affair and later confessed to more transgressions. It's only a month since you found out. Worse still, he's still working with the OW and she's making threats. You've every reason to be anxious!

So what should you do? This is going to sound a bit strange but I think you should embrace your anxiety. Rather than thinking of it as something painful and horrible and to be pushed down as quickly as possible, take some deep breaths and ask yourself: What is my anxiety telling me?

In this case, it's telling you to be prepared for this woman 'attack-ing' you. So think, how could you prepare? Should you talk to your boss to warn him of her? What systems do they have to protect staff from harassment? Do you have a best friend at work who knows and can be ready to pick up the emotional pieces? If you think she will 'attack' at home, what would you do? What about in the street?

Think through all the possibilities and where you could get help.

Next, I'm a bit puzzled. How can she emotionally wound you? Why does her opinion count so much to you? Whatever she might say, she is hardly an unbiased witness! Perhaps you lack confidence and other people's remarks strike home much stronger than they should.

For emergency first aid, if the anxiety gets too much, try this simple breathing exercise. Take a deep breath. Hold it. Say the number ten to yourself. Let out your breath. Repeat but substitute ten for nine and so on down to one and then count back up to ten again.

Finally, when your brain starts to race, pick up a pen and write everything down. Take a look back at your scribblings and cross out everything that's an exaggeration and find the meat (rather than the trimmings of your anxiety) and I bet it will be something important. Once you've isolated it – like with the example of her attacking you – you'll be able to address the issue and move forward.

Why can't I get over my partner's affair? *You need to write down your fears rather than letting them go round and round in your head.*

36. My husband of 40 years has revealed that he's been having an affair with a 30-year-old mature student. The reason he gave was that I kept pushing him away in our marriage and didn't give him the love and affection he needed.

I had no notion whatsoever about the affair. He often worked late as he runs his own business, so I completely trusted him when he told me he needed to spend more time with her because she was about to return to India. I have just lived the past three months in hell. I tried to commit suicide twice. I have beaten him, thrown things at him and called him and her all the names you can think of. I have destroyed his clothes, possessions and I'm absolutely distraught.

I do still love him and he swears he loves me. I need to get a grip and stop hurting him and me or I'm going to lose him forever. The question is HOW? I'm having counselling for depression and stress. I'm also on medication and desperate to put things right.

Andrew writes:

It must have been really hard to write your letter, but I hope you feel better for getting it all out, and reading it back will make you realise just what a dark place you've been in. It's really like you have been negotiating with a gun to his head, you're screaming at him 'make me feel better!' The problem when someone is screaming is that your partner will curl up into a ball and hope you will go away.

I also hope reading back your letter has made you realise that this behaviour is simply not acceptable – you're harming yourself and your marriage. However, the good thing is that you're getting coun-selling and there's a chance to turn the corner and make things better. So, despite the bleakness of your letter, I'm feeling quite positive.

At the core of your problems and your husband's infidelity is the same issue: looking for an instant solution. Let me explain more: when we're in pain – we look for a solution, anything will do, to feel better. The greater the pain, the greater the desire to rid ourselves of it. For example, your husband couldn't cope with the pain of being rejected – so he reached for the easy solution of being 'loved' by this woman (even though she was probably half his age and had a stack of problems of her own). Meanwhile, you couldn't cope with the pain of being rejected either and reached for the instant solution of revenge and destroyed his possessions (even though you know that two wrongs don't make a right). Sadly, you aren't the only people to look for the easy way out – it's why fortunes have been made from brewing alcohol, manufacturing chocolate and creating jewellery – so please be compassionate to yourselves and each other.

So next time you find yourself thinking, 'I'd feel better if only he did this one simple thing', stop and congratulate yourself for spotting an instant solution. More times than not, however, it is a shortcut that's going to get you bogged down in a fresh set of problems. What I'm offering is much harder: learning about yourself, asking for what you need, being able to say 'no' if the request is impossible or costs too much, and finally being able to negotiate a way through these conflicts. The good news is that although these solutions take time, they will endure.

Why can't I get over my partner's affair? *You have been focusing on finding quick fixes which make everything worse rather than better.*

37. My husband had a six-month affair which ended April last year. We made the decision to stay together and try to work things out. We have read many books and this has really helped. When he ended it, he was heartbroken; it was very difficult to stay with someone who was obviously in love with someone else – although he said he loved me also. Nine months on, we have moved house to get away from the area. We have a better relationship than we have had for a few years. We are more honest with each other, more intimate and are enjoying a new life together. He says he is 100 per cent sure he made the right decision to stay with me. We have been married 20 years. My husband is 56, and I am 50. His affair partner was 39 with two young children.

Once his feelings weren't so raw he said he realised it would never have worked with them.

We talked a lot about why it happened; why we had let space grow between us for a third person. My husband was depressed, feeling old and felt like life was over. She showed interest in him, boosted his ego, made him feel good about himself again. I stupidly ignored the signs, had a 'He will snap out of it' attitude. I was also starting to go through the meno-pause, and I had a lot of pain and dryness during sex, which meant our sex life was really bad, but I didn't address this. I have now and we have a very active sex life.

So what's the problem? I still find it difficult to get her out of my head. I drive myself nuts thinking about him having sex with someone else, telling someone else he loved her. When it ended, she was very bitter towards me and sent me emails detailing what they done together, telling me that this would eat away at me for the rest of my life, and I am afraid that this is what is happening. Some days I am OK and I never think about it, but other days I do nothing else but think about it. We have just moved house to start afresh somewhere new and I want this to work more than anything, but I need to stop thinking about it. In your experience, how long does it take for the obsession to stop?

Andrew writes:

Congratulations on the huge progress that you and your husband have made. I am sure that your letter will come as a great inspiration for people who have just discovered an affair – and be proof that things will get better.

As for your problem getting her out of your head, I find this kind of obsession tends to be down to one of the following reasons:

1. *There are questions that you still want to ask.* While trying to row away from disaster, all your energy is focused on recovery and you don't want to bring up any negatives – so you suppress all those little worries and they bind together into a many-headed monster. How do you deal with this? As the affair happened quite a while ago, your husband will be loath to go back over things. However, explain how these questions are torturing you TODAY and how asking these one or two will help.

2. *You have a tendency to over-think.* We are taught that it is good to think through issues, and that's right – up to a point. However, there comes a time where helpful thinking tips over into unhelpful thinking. I am sure that you know when the line has been crossed. Next time, tell yourself: 'That's enough' and distract yourself with something vigorous (like scrubbing the kitchen floor) or something pleasant (like reading a good book).

3. *Unexpressed resentments.* Basically this happens when one partner feels they have shouldered the majority of the burden for getting the relationship on to an even keel again. If this rings true, report your feelings to your husband: 'I'm feeling low because I've been thinking about the affair.' At this point, he could give you a hug, listen to your concerns or maybe apologise again. In this way, you will feel that your hurt has been accepted rather than pushed away.

4. *You might want to punish yourself.* Next time, you start imagining your husband with this woman, stop and ask yourself: 'Why am I torturing myself like this?' Are you angry with yourself for ignoring the signs? Are you angry with yourself for not leaving him and enduring the humiliation of him loving another woman? Are you angry with yourself for getting old and your life 'being over'? Maybe you even enjoy punishing yourself because all the drama makes you feel more alive? It could be none of the above or something else, or maybe simply a habit that you'd like to stop.

Finally, I'd like to talk about the OW and her desire for revenge (by cursing you with the gory details of her sex life). My immediate thought is that she must have been incredibly hurt if she needed to lash out in this way. She must have been desperate if she thought another woman's husband was going to 'save her'. I expect she was crushed by the end of her own marriage, defeated by bringing up two small children alone and terrified of getting older herself. To me, she sounds like a little lost girl (which is rather sad) or angry and out of control (which is rather pathetic). Ultimately, you might like to consider forgiving her – not because she deserves it but as a gift to yourself. If you forgive her, she is out of your life. If you don't, you hold her close as an enemy and keep her around for years to come.

Perhaps you'd like to write an imaginary letter to her. You can put all the hurt she has caused but also add the 'gifts' that she has inadvertently given you: greater understanding of yourself, your husband and a resurrected marriage. I'm not suggesting that you send it but writing everything down could provide a fresh perspective and help move you on.

How long does the recovery process take? I could give you a general figure but I'd like to say: 'It takes what it takes.' What counts is the destination, not how long it takes there. However, the good news is I don't think you have got stuck in Stage Five (Attempted Normality). It sounds like you've done the majority of stage six (Despair-Bodies Float to the Surface) and need just one more push to complete the journey. Going through the first anniversary of discovery is a big landmark event – which will be coming up soon... so be prepared for a couple of difficult days or a small setback. However, the worst is behind you and the road ahead is looking much better. Travel safely.

Why can't I get over my partner's affair? *You need to find compassion for your partner, yourself and even the affair partner.*

WHY AM I DOING ALL THE WORK WHEN MY PARTNER DID ALL THE CHEATING?

38. I am plagued by triggers and flashes of irritability and low moods and wonder whether I will ever feel happy again. Our exclusivity has gone and the lies and deceit are one of the big issues. I wonder what other people feel about the need (which I have) to find the root cause for his affair in order for us both to gain understanding, to reduce a likelihood of another lapse and to find some sort of peace. I have been digging and delving while my husband (who his counsellor says has several defence mechanisms, compartmentalising and internalising, which is difficult to live with) seems able to spend a great deal of time sitting at his computer playing Romans (war game). I'm at a pitch now where I feel fed up with doing all the work to understand him while he has a tendency to say he was overwhelmed and it was a form of escape; a bit of frivolity. He is sorry, guilty, remorseful but still like a rabbit in the headlights. If we could keep everything superficial and bury it I'm sure he would feel OK.

It is a second marriage and there are part-time stepchildren, on both sides, which is an added stress for me. I feel I've spent so much time running around trying to make things fluffy for everyone (I now know it was not my responsibility – my own issues!) that I feel sucked dry and burned out and just want to disconnect and distance myself.

What is the effect of an affair in a second marriage when there are teenage stepchildren as part of the package and difficult dynamics already? I don't know whether we will come through it when he finds it so difficult to talk, to give loving affirmations, etc. Intimacy, we have only managed twice in 11 months post-disclosure. I just feel so low in self-esteem, and trust and respect seem light years away now I've discovered he had not invested fully in our marriage and was disrespectful of my feelings in other ways pre-affair.

He is not the man I thought he was, yet I know deep down he is a good man who did a stupid thing, but my emotions have changed. I had a similar relationship prior to this one – so a double whammy.

Andrew writes:

I'm afraid it's a common dilemma: you've been hurt and betrayed by your partner so you'd think he'd do everything in his power to help you feel better. However, he's putting his head in the sand (or deep in his computer game) and you're doing all the work. It feels like a double betrayal. You have my complete sympathy because it's not fair. However, as I type those words I can hear my mother's voice saying: 'Who said life is fair? It's not, and you'd better get used to it!' I know these are wise words but they're not much comfort, so let's try and look at things from a different perspective.

I believe that we are all responsible for own lives and that means when we get hurt, we're responsible for our own healing. Of course, you can have help from a therapist, your partner and your friends, but ultimately it's up to you to make sense of what happened, find answers that resonate for you and make the necessary changes.

After an affair, it helps to think of three boxes. In the first, there are all *your* problems. In the second, there's all *his* problems. In the third, there are your *relationship's* problems. You're not responsible for opening his box – only he can do that. At the moment, it sounds like he'd rather keep the lid firmly shut and that's his prerogative. However, you ARE responsible for your box. Fortunately you've started to unpack the contents and have spotted that you've been busy solving everybody else's stuff and neglecting your own. So what else could be in your box?

I think the most interesting comment of your post is right at the end. 'I had a similar relationship prior to this one.' It is tempting to think, 'He won't talk' and 'Why am I wasting my time' and 'there's someone better suited to me out there'. But if you don't sort out your material, you're likely to go out and do it for a third time! Trust me, you don't want that. So instead of hoping he will change, look at your own issues? Why do you have to make everything fluffy for other people? Could you give yourself some of the loving affirmations – rather than feed everybody else and feel drained? What about your childhood makes it hard to ask for what you need and hope everybody else will guess and give it you?

Finally, we have your relationship box and the good news here is that you're only responsible for half of it. What would happen if you learnt to communicate better? What would it take to restore intimacy again in your relationship? Have you been giving your husband all the responsibility for initiating sex? What would help you relax and enjoy sex? Could you ask for it?

So focus on what you can change rather than be angry for what you can't and my hope is that it will kick-start your recovery – either with or without him.

Why can't I get over my partner's affair? *You're focusing on how life should be rather than dealing with the reality of how it is.*

39.

I have just finished reading *My Wife Doesn't Love Me Any More*, as just over three weeks ago my wife of ten years told me she wasn't attracted to me or in love with me any more. I initially reacted badly, doing all the wrong things out of utter panic and fear for the future and for what would happen to me and our two-and-a-half-year-old daughter.

Thankfully, your book and other articles have really helped me change my response and realise the damage I was doing. There has been a dramatic improvement in our relationship since I changed my behaviours and started focusing on being a better person for me as well as for the sake of our relationship.

While I recognise that this is going to be a long process, I am prepared for that and can remain positive for the most part. However, I have recently found out that she has been texting another man who she met on a night out with her friends the weekend before she told me about falling out of love. We have discussed the situation calmly and without getting upset or angry, which has helped and she appears to have been totally honest, even to the point of admitting that she has arranged to meet him next weekend for a drink.

I'm now feeling confused, although all I want in the world is to win my wife back and to work on making our relationship stronger and more fulfilled than ever before (not that she is in the same place). I don't think I can allow her to meet up with someone else; I am considering telling her that I want her to cancel her plans to meet him and make a decision whether or not to work on our relationship. However, if she isn't willing to cancel their meeting, I will have to leave her in order to protect myself from more hurt and out of respect for myself.

Do I have any other option?

Andrew writes:

First off, I want to congratulate you on the progress made since reading *My Wife Doesn't Love Me Any More*. Well done also for discussing the other man calmly and getting an honest answer.

So, do you have any other options, beyond ordering her to cancel the meeting and leaving her? I know this is painful and eating you up inside but I think you're falling into a common trap. I call it fix or flee. In other words, you need immediate certainty to feel safe (even if the result is not what you want).

Instead, I want you to stare in the darkness and stand firm; slowly but surely you'll discover a bit of grey rather than just black and white. After all, going for a drink with someone – even to whom you are attracted – does not necessarily mean you're going to start an affair with them! Your wife could discover, he's nice but not all that. She might discover he's got more problems than the Queen has jewels (and she doesn't really want to deal with a jealous ex-wife and three daughters who demand his attention round the clock, etc). There are lots of other possibilities.

You could also be assertive and ASK her to cancel rather than NOT ALLOW (your words). It would be even more powerful if you reported your feelings too. So something like... 'I'm really uncomfortable about you going for a drink with another man, would you consider cancelling it?' Don't put on the heavy pressure about the effect on your daughter or make threats as this will just make you come across as controlling (not a good look). If she says NO, ask her why not? Listen, ask more questions and discuss. Ultimately, it is much better if she decides from her own free will not to go rather being banned from seeing him. (I doubt that's what you mean but that's how it's coming across in your letter and that will put her back up and make her more determined to go!)

If it does develop into a relationship, that's the moment to move out (and protect yourself), but you're thinking 17 steps ahead. Concentrate on the here and now and use this as a chance to show that you can communicate effectively rather than threaten or emotionally blackmail. Your wife texting another man does not have to mean the end of working on your relationship; it's just an obstacle (sadly a rather common one) on the road ahead.

Why can't I get over my partner's affair? *You're setting an arbitrary test for your partner about how committed she is to your relationship and setting her and yourself up for failure.*

40. Out of the blue, my husband of ten years, announced he was unhappy, moved out and moved to Germany – all in the space of two weeks. Within six weeks he had already started a new relationship with a work colleague (someone he has known for four years!). We are now at the six-month mark.

Our marriage, towards the end, was not easy. We had a myriad issues – poor sex life, constant arguing and challenging each other, complete lack of communication, etc – all exacerbated by my husband working in Germany most of the week and me juggling two young children (aged two and four) and a stressful job.

I have read several of your books but my husband has no interest in talking. In his mind, he has made the decision and that's that. But I am struggling. I have reflected on my own behaviour during the past year of our marriage and have made positive changes to how I react, and behave towards my husband. I am focusing on myself and the children and am learning to become content with what I've got rather than what I don't have. Despite all of this, I can't let go. I still love my husband dearly. When we spend time together, we laugh, we enjoy the children and it feels so right to me. I still feel hopeful, despite him being with someone else. I keep telling myself to be patient, focus on myself and keep being positive towards him. My friends tell me I'm crazy, that I deserve some-one better, etc. Am I kidding myself? I feel so confused.

Andrew writes:

My first reaction is that you have to go at the pace that feels right for you – not your friends. If you want to stay where you are, that's fine. You'll move on to the next stage – whatever that may be – when you're good and ready. (Friends want us better straight away so look for instant answers – 'dump him' or 'seduce him' – but real, lasting solutions take much longer.) If you and your partner are getting on well and the children are benefiting, that sounds like a really good place to be at the moment.

If you want to work on improving your communication – which is beneficial whether you stay together or not (as you will still need to cooperate as parents) – it doesn't matter if he doesn't like to 'talk'. You don't need hours of pouring over what went wrong, you can improve your marriage small interaction by small interaction. Most men get ILYB because they swallow their feelings and are not assertive (telling their partner what they want in a straightforward way). Sadly, some women prefer to get their own way or think their way is right and don't truly listen (or more likely in your case, did not understand the depth of your husband's unhappiness). So next time there's a problem remember my mantra for being assertive: *I can ask, you can say and we can negotiate.*

However, while you're working hard on changing yourself and your marriage, your husband has gone for an instant solution: 'new love', and under the power of limerence (the walking on air stage at the beginning of a romance) believes that he has found the answer to all his prayers. It's pointless to try and reason with him. So don't waste your breath with getting angry. Sadly, the myths of love and all the messages from movies and popular songs that 'love changes everything' and 'with you, I'm born again' gives us unrealistic expectations. So when your wife is angry, preoccupied with two small children and hasn't had sex for six months, you can start to think she doesn't love you any more (because otherwise she'd make you a priority) and that the only answer is to find someone who does care. Fortunately, his sky-high expectations, that love will solve all his problems, will impact on his new 'relationship' too. When the shine wears off, he will discover he has all the same issues – not able to communicate effectively or ask for what he needs – plus a whole lot of guilt and grief from his new woman (who doesn't understand why he needs to spend so much time with his kids). At this point, he might be ready to start working on your marriage or he might blindly press on and look for 'new' love number two, three, four, etc.

I'm afraid I can't predict which way it will go but if you change, the dynamic of your relationship will change and that opens the door to trying again. Shutting down, telling yourself you 'deserve' better and getting angry just builds a wall between you and makes it harder to start over.

Why can't I get over my partner's affair? *It's OK to be in limbo at the moment – especially if you're still learning and growing.*

41. I found out that my husband had an affair (for four weeks) with one of my best and oldest friends. When I asked him about it he said it had been only one kiss and that they had written emails. He first thought he had fallen in love, but it was over now. I believed him and told him I wanted him to have no more contact with her. When I asked him for the reason he said he had been very unhappy in our relationship. We are both 40, we have been a couple for 18 years and married for six years, with two children (aged three and six). Two years ago we had moved to a new place because my husband started a new job. I was at home with the children. I had health problems, I was really exhausted and had no one there to talk to, no relatives and no friends, so I became depressed; I suffered from panic attacks and could not, for example, even drive by car to the nearest city. My husband helped me a lot, but it became a burden for him. Furthermore, we did not talk very much to each other and rarely had sex. Therefore, I could understand why he had taken the opportunity to have an affair when it was offered (before we got married, I had an email affair myself and know how you can get addicted).

Although it was tough for me to be betrayed by an old friend of mine, when I found out, it was like a wake-up call for me. He was still the love of my life, and my family was so important for me, so I absolutely wanted to save this and changed my habits. I paid him more attention and became interested in his life and work and cared for him; I became more independent, I looked after my health and started to work out and have therapy for my depression. He said he wanted to save our relationship too, so we made a plan of what we could do for our relationship and for ourselves. We talked a lot, and our sex life became better than ever.

I read your book *How Can I Ever Trust You Again?* and it helped me a lot. I thought we had reached 'Attempted Normality' after nearly two months when I found out that he had started the affair again. He had 'said' that he had broken ties with her, but only a few days later he'd written to her again (just to ask how she was) and they soon started the affair anew.

I finally got him to tell me everything. It had not only been the one kiss, they had sex too. He had really been clever to hide his tracks – had a second email account and met her on business trips. This was a real shock for me. I had the impression that we were on to a good thing and that we had a good chance to save our relationship. He had promised me so much and I had done everything I could! I thought we were happy again! He said, it had not been for nothing, that with all my efforts he had found out that he could have a great life with me and that he loved me again; he just did not find a way to end the affair. When he finally said that he loved me again he had ended the affair, but on that same day I found out about a credit card bill. He said he did not even love her and sex was bad. He had written to her to say that he loved her because she wanted to hear that from him, but he did not mean it. But he cannot understand how he could do all that, and how he could break all his principles.

Somehow I could have lived with the first part of the affair. But it hurts me so much that he could not keep his promise and cheated on me again. The first time, I could understand, but later he was not lacking anything and said he was happy with me again. So why did he do that? And why couldn't he end it earlier? If sex was bad and she was not his type and he did not love her, then why did he go to bed with her? Whenever I touch him (and I can barely do that, I can't even think of kissing him) I can see her face, wonder what they had been doing together and imagine them having sex. All the little gestures and things we had, with everything I wonder if they shared it too. He says it is over, he only wants me and our family, but I cannot believe him anymore. I live in anxiety that he will start to cheat on me again. What can I do?

Andrew writes:

I'm afraid to tell you that this scenario is all too common. So why do men, who seem to be sorting everything out, start up their affair all over again? I'll do my best to explain because I've counselled quite a lot of these men, and I have a fairly good idea of what's going on in their heads.

After an affair, the Discovered realises that they have let everybody down: their partner, their children and themselves. The full impact of their behaviour (which has been kept at bay by rationalising, compartmentalising and minimising) hits them between the eyes and they are full of shame. I know you're going to say, 'Hurrah' and 'Perhaps they won't do it again', but shame is the most toxic of all emotions. This is because it's the opposite of love and we feel unworthy and full of despair. We talk colloquially of 'dying of shame' and it's not really an exaggeration (and why ancient societies used exile as the most powerful of punishments).

On a day-to-day basis, it is possible to cope with shame – by telling yourself 'I'm going to make things up to my partner'. However, recovery never runs smoothly. There are days when the Discovered's partner is besieged by crying jags or something triggers anger (perhaps discovering an old text or a small row about the children escalates); all the hope disappears and the Discovered is overwhelmed by shame again. Unfortunately, there's only so much shame that anyone can cope with. At this point, these men have an intense desire to feel OK again. So they reach for the drug that made them feel 'good' in the past and have a sneaky peak at the OW's Facebook site. Perhaps they feel shame about hurting the affair partner too. So they attempt to assuage this guilt – for example by sending a message like 'I hope you're OK?' – which allows the ex-affair partner to get her/his hooks in all over again. Before too long, shame triggers bad behaviour and an even deeper amount of shame, which needs an even bigger hit to escape and the whole shameful affair starts again. Not surprisingly, it doesn't bring much joy, and rather like an alcoholic looking back at a night in the gutter or lying in their own vomit in the hallway, they can't explain why they acted so stupidly.

I know you're going to be full of questions. For example: when I feel shame, I don't act out like this? Not every man who is unfaithful lets shame get the better of him and plunges back into the affair. So why is my husband so weak? Taking the first question, most men don't have intimate friends with whom they can share their problems and feel less alone. Most women have sympathetic girlfriends to share the load, help them understand their pain and ultimately feel less shamed. Sadly, men are socialised to be self-reliant and sort their own problems (for fear of being seen as weak). Therefore, they tend to have sports buddies or business associates. It is OK for men to open up about emotional problems to their wives but they have hurt her and she is probably reinforcing their feelings of shame. There is, however, one other candidate. Yes, you've guessed it, the affair partner, and in desperation, or a vulnerable moment, he will turn to her.

Next, let's look at why your husband is so vulnerable to shame or as you might put it, so 'weak'! (I hope you might spot how this sort of language would shame him further and exacerbate a tricky situation.) Sadly, some parents – who are uncomfortable with strong feelings – unwittingly teach their children: 'Don't think and don't feel'. So when these sons (and daughters) get upset, they say things like 'Don't make a fuss' or 'Pull yourself together' or by their actions pass on an unspoken message that feelings are unacceptable and everything should be kept 'nice'. (In a way, these silent instructions are even more powerful.) Unfortunately, if you don't learn how to accept your emotions as a child, you end up with two options as an adult: 'unemotional / closed down until the pressure is too much and then shatter all over the place' or 'over-emotional and not able to differentiate between real and imagined threats and therefore are forever 'flying off the handle'.

There is another possible scenario that could explain your husband's behaviour. Some parents use shame to control their children and metaphorically (or literally) turn their backs and withdraw their love if their son (or daughter) does something of which they disapprove. Not surprisingly, these children grow up full of shame and only the tiniest drop will push them over the edge and overwhelm them.

At this point, you're probably overwhelmed yourself, but there is a silver lining. The shock of his original bad behaviour compounded by even worse behaviour, not being able to explain his actions and realising that he doesn't understand himself provides an opportunity. To paraphrase the singer songwriter Leonard Cohen (from his song 'Anthem'): 'It's the cracks that let the light in', and your husband has certainly been cracked wide open! You'll find that he will be happy to get some form of therapy to understand the full impact of his childhood, learn about his emotions and ultimately to befriend rather than run away from them.

Why can't I get over my partner's affair? *Affairs are often made up of many layers of deception – each of which needs to be made sense of and worked through.*

HOW CAN WE WORK ON OUR RELATIONSHIP WHEN MY PARTNER IS DEPRESSED AND OVERWHELMED WITH GUILT?

42. I recently found out that my husband of five years (together for nine, we also have four young children ranging between six and five months) had sex with an ex-student of his three times over the course of six months. I had been paranoid about this girl for some time, but he always denied anything. Apparently he finished it, but six months later when they bumped into each other he walked with her, hugged her, kissed her, had sex and then ended it again. However, she still texted him and they continued to text each other and get really flirty. I found the messages nine months ago and confronted him but he denied it again. I emailed this girl at the time, but heard nothing. Out of the blue, two months ago, she emailed me back and said she had something to tell me. I asked him about it and he finally confessed to it.

After much discussing and shouting, he finally stated that there were four reasons why he did it:

1. Our marriage (I have never really shown him any love, or affection, haven't told him that I loved him for about six years) and I control everything.

2. Pressures at work.

3. Outside interference from family (my side), not feeling that our marriage is private.

4. The death of his mother three years ago and for whom he never grieved.

My husband claims that he does not recognise the person that did what he did, that he did not have any feelings for her, that he didn't enjoy it and that he deeply regrets it. He was signed off from work and is currently seeking professional help – being diagnosed as suffering from depression. His therapist has claimed that he has been mentally ill.

I have been able to sit back and look at our marriage and hold my hands up to my faults, and I can recognise that many of my difficulties stem from issues not related to my husband. However, some are related to him and unresolved issues from the beginning of our relationship. I have bought *How Can I Ever Trust You Again?* and *I Love You But...* and have found both books to be brilliant.

I am terrified that my husband will do this again and absolutely do not trust him. My problem is mainly that I don't know what to believe because he so blatantly lied to me. When he was sleeping with her, I thought things were fine (but he claims that he was masking everything and making out everything was fine to stop conflict at home).

Is it possible for someone to suffer mentally to a degree that they can cheat? Is it possible for someone to have an affair and yet not have feelings for that person or enjoy some element of the affair? If my husband regretted it each time, then why would he go back? And if he ended it each time, what makes the last time he ended it any different? I feel that when he goes back to work it could all happen again – how can I learn to move past this? I am also struggling in that I find the slightest thing reminds me of the situation and brings the pain back to the surface – please help.

Andrew writes:

Let's take a deep breath and work through your questions.

Yes. It is possible to have an affair and not be in love or even enjoy it very much. If your husband was desperate, depressed and saw no future in anything, he would have done almost anything to get out of that hole. Someone coming along and saying 'I love you' and 'You're wonderful' and 'Let me give you a momentary high from hot sex' seems like the answer to your prayers. However, it's a bit like someone offering a gallon tub of ice cream or a bottle of whisky. It takes the pain away for a while but you feel terrible the next day! Did you really enjoy the ice cream or whisky – not very much? Worse still, you feel terrible shame and sink lower and become even more vulnerable to the next offer of cheap sex, ice cream or whisky.

Can you suffer mentally to the point that you start cheating? Certainly if your husband has manic depression, it is not uncommon to cheat in the manic phase. (Quite a few people are diagnosed in the aftermath of an affair.)

You're frightened it will happen again. Of course, that's only natural. Same with the slightest things reminding you of the affair. I'm not surprised you've been on high alert for months and months; it will take time to feel safe again.

However, there is lots of good news. If you attend to your half of the problem and learn to communicate properly (rather than demand or control), he will learn to ask for what he needs (rather than bottle and blow). Your husband could start to grieve for his mother – rather than deny and push the feelings to one side. You can both change, grow and have a better relationship. So next time there is adversity you will tackle it together (rather than your husband feeling he's on his own).

Why can't I get over my partner's affair? *Your recovery might not feel secure but you're making really good progress.*

43.

It's been a year since I discovered my husband of five years was having an inappropriate friendship. He confessed ILYB but was willing to give our relationship another go. He said he would break contact with her. I spent the next few months giving our relationship 100 per cent, learning from your books, trying to understand his perspective and to listen fully. I also made sure I was stating clearly what I wanted, ie a full, committed, relationship with him, and more input in me and family life (we have a three-year-old son).

In late autumn, I discovered he'd gone away with his 'friend' for a couple of days, saying he was away for work. I was devastated yet again. He said he should leave and I agreed, although asked him to stop, take stock and consider everything so we could make suitable arrangements. Christmas came and went and I expected him to leave but he didn't. He is still sleeping on the sofa and there has been no relationship other than a functional one around family life for four months now.

I have stated I would consider being with him if he stopped all contact with his friend and committed fully to trying again. However, whenever we talk he deflects any decisions. He permanently sits on the fence saying he thinks the world of me, but won't actually commit to being with me or leaving. I have stated I either want to be with him if we are both committed to improving our relationship, or I want to get on with my life apart from him. He won't attend counselling with me or alone although I have undertaken some. I have given this so much time and effort as I love him and we have a son. I can't understand his inability to either choose a direction, or commit to exploring how he feels through counselling.

I have given a year of my life to trying to improve things, but it takes two. I don't feel I have any more to give, without receiving more back from him. It's got to the point I feel rundown, emotionally exhausted and ambivalent. I feel upset about the situation, angry with his behaviour and angry that it may be left to me to decide because he won't stay properly or leave. I want more from life and I'm not getting it! I'm not a quitter but I don't want to waste my time over someone who isn't there for me.

Andrew writes:

One of the toughest scenarios with infidelity is when the Discovered goes into a deep shock after their affair or 'friendship' is revealed. Although they know their behaviour is wrong, they have protected themselves from considering the full impact through minimising ('My partner is so angry all the time, I don't think she or he really cares so they won't be too hurt') or compartmentalising ('This is just for me and won't have any impact on anyone else' and 'She won't find out' or 'He can't find out') or excusing ('Love is like an invading army and you can do nothing but surrender'). In most cases, these are really kind and generous men and women who put others first, have strong moral values and seldom think of their own needs. Their partners often say, 'He was the last person I thought would have an affair' or 'It goes against everything that she believes in'. So when their partner is racked with pain and crying for hours on end, not only are all the justifications and weasel-like formulas that allow people to cheat stripped bare and revealed as pitiful but the Discovered has to confront the baseness of their own nature.

In some cases, it can be the spur to learning and growing but often they tip from shock into depression. Maybe they have been suffering from low-level depression for years and holding it at bay by a combination of keeping busy, distracting themselves and denying their unhappy feelings. Perhaps the affair was another coping strategy to help them 'feel alive' again because the rawness of the feelings around infidelity can kick-start the emotions – a bit like putting a defibrillator across the heart and shocking it into beating. However, after the discovery of the affair, they are facing all sorts of horrible feelings: shame, guilt, remorse, etc. They have no experience of facing such overwhelming emotions, have no helpful coping strategies, or everybody in their family will be shocked, horrified or disappointed and therefore can't be told.

Even if the discovered has not been borderline depressed, it is very easy to tip from ashamed into feeling depressed and on into full clinical depression – where someone has trouble functioning. In many ways, I'm surprised that more Discovered people don't become depressed as the roots of depression and affairs are in the same soil. Let me explain, by giving two statements about depression:

1. Depression is caused by suppression (you start by denying the unwelcome feelings but as you can't pick and choose, you end up switching them all off).

2. Depression is caused by anger turned inwards.

And here are two statements about affairs:

1. Affairs are caused by suppressing your needs (and going along with what other people want) – which tips into resentment and believing one is 'entitled' to some happiness.

2. Affairs are caused by anger turned outwards – all the failings of the partner are listed and exaggerated but instead of addressing them

(in a positive manner) they are used to justify cheating. When the affair is discovered, the Discovered turns this anger on him or herself.

Therefore, it is perfectly possible that your partner is depressed and overwhelmed with guilt. I have to say I don't think he has made full disclosure yet. It makes no sense to me that this was 'only' an inappropriate affair (ie, no sex) because men do not lie and go away with 'friends' for a couple of days and not have some form of sexual relations with them. It sounds like he is still suppressing both the truth and his feelings – and thereby feeding his depression.

In an ideal world, he would confess to what has really gone on (and allow you to make an informed choice), he would go to his doctor and discuss medication (to help provide a base line of feeling OK) and have some therapy like CBT (cognitive behavioural therapy) to challenge some of his most negative thought patterns. However, I'm aware that we don't live in an ideal world and he will probably refuse to seek help.

However, that doesn't stop you from taking care of yourself, continuing to seek help and learning from the situation. I hope understanding that your husband might be ill will allow you to be compassionate as well as angry (which is not going to help lift his depression).

Why can't I get over my partner's affair? *He is suffering from a mental illness and is currently unable to face the enormity of what he has done.*

44. My marriage has been suffering for some years. Neither my husband nor I knew how to take positive steps towards working through the issues. We both knew something was wrong but didn't even know how to say, 'How are YOU feeling? What shall we do?'

After eight years of being married, we had a beautiful baby girl. Around the time our daughter's first birthday I think we both started to be depressed. With sleep patterns being restored, we thought life would get back to 'normal', but that was a mirage.

We live in Japan and have been traumatised with the earthquakes and the nuclear crisis. My husband moved us to the western part of the country (to avoid aftershocks and possible radioactive contamination) and his company has a few branch offices, so the idea was to stay at our new home four days a week, and the rest in his studio in Tokyo, close to his office.

When my daughter and I initially departed Tokyo, my husband left us at the gate, telling us that in fact he needed to stay to man the ship. I felt abandoned. The summer was spent apart – with three or four visits to where my daughter and I were. I was stressed in a new environment and dealing with the post-trauma shock. I could not tend to my husband's emotional needs – I was barely keeping it together for me and my daughter. When he would visit, I could not tend to his physical needs either, because I felt the only time he wanted to touch me was to have sex.

So begins the emotional and physical jet lag – neither of us were in the same time zone at a given time. As you can guess, the marriage suffered. After moving into our new home, it was hell. There was no more conversation. Just sighing and eye rolling. It was terrible. After three months of this, I was at my wits end and wrote a long letter detailing what was not working, and that we should consider splitting up if we could work it out. I had been very unhappy, and just short of telling him ILYB for a very long time.

Just before Christmas, he told me ILYB, and that he needed to experiment outside of the marriage. I knew resisting would just make him go deeper and faster into the affair, so I told him why I didn't agree, that I can't tell him what to do or not to do – that I will stand by him while he chooses to deal with our problems this way. I told him that I see it like those life-altering events that either makes or breaks a marriage – like losing a child or a terminal illness.

Things seemed to get better with better communication and enjoying each other's company in February, but he told me that he is having an affair. He just needed to get it off his chest – he has shown no signs that he wanted to end it. He will not touch me with a ten-foot pole, but will only hug and kiss me like a child.

So to recap – initially, it was me in the ILYB situation and wanting to leave, but I wanted to work on the relationship before deciding.

I finally told him in a very cruel way ILYB, and I guess he was hurt. I don't know whether it's out of revenge, or out of seeking affirmation (or both – he says he doesn't know why he's doing it aside from the sexual gratification), he just lashed out and left and is now telling me ILYB.

I betrayed him with money (though I do think it's unfair on his part, as everything was transparent and I always asked him for his approval on large purchases – I think it's more about resentment for recently becoming the sole breadwinner – though that too, he decided when he evacuated us from Tokyo) and now he is betraying me with the affair.

I am afraid the longer he stays in the affair, the more complicated it is going to be for everyone – but I know I'm the last person he's going to want to hear it from.

If he could just break up with the OW so that we can attempt to resolve our differences, I will be at peace if it doesn't work out in the end. At least we will have given our relationship a chance.

His father is now very ill. He grew up with a bitter single mother who has repeatedly told him that he was not wanted. There is a lot of turmoil in his family and no one is on 'normal' speaking terms. Just screaming matches. So as far as father figures go, he has a poor role model.

So... how do you recommend working through all of this – the initial betrayal (I am changing my relationship with money through a correspondence course), the emotional jet lag, getting him to come back to the table so we can try to work things out?

Andrew writes:

It sounds like you've both been through a terrible time. You are both exhausted, shocked and desperately in need of being held. Unfortunately, the events of the last few months have pushed you both further apart and made it harder to reach out to each other. In many ways, I'm not surprised. One of the main impacts of trauma – and they don't get much bigger than an earthquake and nuclear disaster – is to make people shut down emotionally and retreat into themselves. (Especially if they have had trauma of some kind in the past.)

It sounds like your husband had a self-medicating or cry for help affair – in a desperate attempt to feel a little better. Although you are not responsible for your husband's infidelity, you are one half of the marriage and allowed it to degenerate to this point. Think about what you regret and think about making an fulsome apology for your half. By this I mean 'I am sorry that I did x, I am aware that it must have made you feel y', and then explain what changes you are going to make to ensure it does not happen again. I know it is tempting to explain why you behaved in this way. However, this can be heard as justifying your behaviour and lessens the impact of the apology. This strategy will certainly get his attention – because he will be expecting more recriminations – and hopefully, it will encourage him to do something similar.

On to his father's illness, if you can be kind – and the opposite of the screaming matches he had at home – you could become his support again (rather than the enemy). Always remember he comes from a home where aggression and shouting is normal. My guess is that he is so carefully attuned to conflict that he will hear a lion roar when there is only a mouse squeak. So what you saw as a letter trying to fix things – but detailing the problems – he could have heard as an attack.

I know it all sounds bleak. So let's move on to the positives. You have a daughter together and eight years of marriage to fall back on. You also have a good attitude: 'I will do what I can to save this marriage but if it doesn't work out, I will survive.'

If you want to save your relationship, you are going to have be patient and calm. Instead of trying to get him back at the table to 'work on your relationship' or trying to force him to give up the OW, I would concentrate on feeling stronger yourself and being in a better place. I would also look at improving your day-to-day communication, for example over your daughter. Slowly but surely, the atmosphere between the two of you will improve. He will begin to be less defensive and I think realise that this OW is not going to make him happy. That's when the real work can begin. In the meantime, you will have to live with uncertainty (but the alternative is pushing for certainty and getting more eye-rolling).

Why can't I get over my partner's affair? *You need to focus on taking care of yourself at the moment rather than healing your marriage.*

45.

I am at my wits end and feel I'm going nowhere. I have read at least three of your books so far, *I Love You But I'm Not in Love with You*, *My Wife Doesn't Love Me Any More* and *How Can I Ever Trust You Again?* and while they have been helpful to me I am still in a horrible position. The main problem I have is that nowhere can I find a scenario that relates to my situation. All the books I have read (I have also read other people's) refer to resolving problems and arguments, but my wife and I don't have any such problems.

I will try to summarise a very complicated and long story into a short one. About four years ago, a friend of mine approached my wife to instigate an affair. My wife is outwardly a very flirty, almost attention-seeking woman who does come over to men as being 'up for it', for want of a better expression. Whenever we are out she is surrounded by men like bees to a honey pot (she is also very attractive, which helps of course). He obviously thought he had a shot at a 'bit on the side', as he too is married with a family. She told him she loved me and that she didn't want to meet. Then in a state of shock contacted me to tell me what had happened. She asked me not to contact him and said she would deal with the problem, to which I reluctantly and stupidly agreed.

For a while there was a series of text and phone conversations that she told me about whereby she told him that nothing was going to happen, until one day I discovered that she had contacted him and not only didn't tell me but actually avoided telling me. At this stage, the picture had obviously changed and I could no longer wait for her to deal with the situation, so I confronted them both. He apologised and said it would never happen again and stressed that nothing had happened other than conversations. My wife at this point came out with the ILYB statement for the first time; however, it was agreed we would try to sort things out.

Unfortunately, over the following three years, they did begin a full-blown affair where they met up regularly and while they never had full intercourse, she did regularly perform sexual acts for him. During this time, our relationship appeared to go through highs and lows, which I can now relate to the fact that the affair was broken off by him on several occasions because he wanted to 'do the right thing'. I assume the lower points in our relationship would equate to the times when the affair was rekindled.

During this time I assumed the problems were just due to ILYB until eventually her behaviour became so obvious that I started to look more closely and finally confronted her. At this time, I did not believe he was involved as we had spoken. I had believed him when he said it wouldn't happen again. I had forgiven him and we had continued to be friends, although never in quite the same way. However, it did turn out to be him and once again I had to confront him, this time with no possibility of forgiveness.

This was over a year ago and my wife is still here in body if not in spirit. Since the affair ended she has refused point blank to accept what she did was wrong and will apparently never apologise for it, although she has apologised for the pain that it has caused. For months and months she pined after this man, lying in bed crying if we happened to drive past him in the opposite direction and caught a glimpse of him and I know she has told a friend on several occasions she has had to fight the urge to email him.

As for us, we just celebrated our 20th wedding anniversary; we get on really well, are such good friends and do lots of things together. We have always had a very active and excellent sex life, although this has changed somewhat lately. Prior to the affair we were one of those inseparable couples who would never dream of not doing things together. This was a two-way thing and not at all one-sided; she would always want to come with me to things that weren't of real interest to her just so we could be together. If she went anywhere she would always ask me to come. Life was on the whole very good. Even now, externally things seem fine, she is happy and chirpy, we cuddle a lot and still do everything together. We don't argue and the only times things become awkward are when this subject comes up.

She doesn't really ever want to talk or discuss the situation but still feels there is something missing and that it's not fair that she stays. I believe she has decided to go but is waiting until after we go on holiday in July. We tried counselling, but after a couple of individual sessions the counsellor thought we shouldn't have couples sessions as we were not yet both looking for the same outcome. I wanted to fix things but my wife just wanted to discover if she wanted to stay or not. My wife says that she wished she could sort things out but she still can't bring herself to say she wants to try and fix things, so we are stuck in horrible limbo where I want to correct whatever went wrong and I can't seem to get her to want to try... although she insists she is trying very hard!!!

I am so confused and lost. I'm trying so hard to keep this from our children who are not young but still live at home and would be devastated if she left, as of course would I.

Andrew writes:

I think your wife is mourning for her 'lost love'. She is full of guilt and shame and that's why she doesn't want to talk to you. The guilt and shame will also probably make her build the affair up into something it wasn't: 'I was swept away by a wave of feelings' or 'We were right for each other' because that makes her feel less guilty. Therefore, in her mind, she wasn't 'responsible' for her feelings. She was 'taken over' by them. The alternative is just too bleak to think about, ie I had a cheap little affair.

None of this helps you move forward because trying to convince her that this was not the love of her life will just make you into the enemy.

Underneath all of this I wonder if she's lost her purpose in life. If you've been together for 20 years, my guess is that the children are growing up and they don't need her so much. If she's a very outgoing, flirty sort of person, I bet that appearances are very important to her. How does she feel about being in her 40s? She really needs to take time to find a new reason for getting up in the morning. However, this is something that she's got to do for herself; you can't force her into it. You can be supportive, available to talk to, but if you keep pestering her all the time she will keep you at arms' length. So I'm afraid we're still in the age of uncertainty.

You need to keep doing positive things to support yourself and learn to communicate effectively rather than simply avoid arguments. Your wife's natural tendency is to agree to what other people want – for example, going to your events even if they don't interest her. However, you need to be individuals as well as a couple, 'I' as well as 'we'. So I would double-check she truly wants to come: 'Are you sure?' I would give her permission to say no: 'You don't need to come to please me'. You could also trade, if she does still insist: 'Is there something I could do for you in return?' In this way, you would be pointing her in the direction of assertiveness: helping her to say no and encouraging negotiating (when your desires or needs clash).

Finally, I want you to take the pressure off yourself, your wife and your relationship. I know limbo is unpleasant but it's much better than sweeping everything under the carpet (like you did three years ago by agreeing to 'sort everything out' but actually changing nothing). Limbo is also better than pushing for certainty – which at the moment is that your wife is in mourning and possibly depressed too. Unable to see a way forward, she will offer splitting up as the solution. Limbo can buy time to improve your communication. Finally, it's OK to get angry with each other from time to time. An argument doesn't have to be a screaming match but it will bring issues to the surface and create an urgency to change.

Why can't I get over my partner's affair? *You need to own up to the depth of the problems between the two of you.*

HOW DO I FORGIVE?

46. I knew my wife and I were having problems and were growing emotionally and sexually distant because I was a bit jealous and controlling. I think I was this way because my ex-wife had cheated on me. My current wife has told me she felt like she could never earn my trust and had never had it since the start of our relationship. She told me she thought she wanted a divorce and began staying with a friend.

After about a month she came home and said she realised she loved me and wanted to work it out. She kept staying with her girlfriends and going out though, and acting distant. I did some research by checking her Facebook and found out she slept with another man while she was drunk. She then slept with him a second time sober to see if there was something there. The second time she felt disgusted and sad. She said it made her miss me and realise she loved me and had messed up our marriage and that is why she couldn't come home and face me.

We are trying hard to get over this but I'm having trouble forgetting that my wife slept with another man. Please help me with some advice.

Andrew writes:

My advice is simple: don't forget! You are having those thoughts and feelings for a good reason. In effect, there was something wrong with your relationship and in particular your behaviour that needs to change.

Lots of men try and sweep problems under the carpet – which is impossible – or blank out their pain by going into a new relationship (which you did last time and just brought the suspicion into this relationship). However, this time, I'd like to think that you're going to face the pain: learn from this experience, understand why you're particularly prone to jealousy and make a commitment to change.

First off, I'd like you to apologise to your wife for being controlling and letting the past poison your love for her. Next, I'd like you to write down all the reasons why you can't forgive – both your first wife and second wife. I expect you'll write things down like: 'it excuses bad behaviour' or 'she might do it again' or 'she doesn't deserve to be forgiven' or 'she needs to meet certain conditions first'. What's on your list? I think you'll find that this exercise will inflame your anger, make you feel helpless and increase the distance between you and your wife.

But what would happen if you decided to forgive your first wife? I hope it will lighten your load, because holding on to your anger is not going to hurt your ex. (It's a bit like drinking poison and expecting the other person to die.) She has long since moved on, forgotten or simply dismissed you as a bitter old man. We think forgiveness is a feeling but really it's a decision. You can tell yourself: 'It's time to forgive.' Trust me, you will feel a whole lot better.

Moving on to your current wife, I want you to listen to what the last few years have been like and the impact of your behaviour on her. Don't explain or justify your actions but instead use the three most powerful words in the recovery skill box: tell me more. Afterwards, apologise for what you regret and it will probably encourage her to make a similar apology too. It might also be a step towards forgiving her (at some point in the future).

Finally, I'd like you to understand yourself better. Why do feel the need to control? Did you have controlling parents? Did they let you down badly and make you feel powerless as a child? If you can see the bigger picture, it might be possible to forgive yourself and that's a big step forward.

Why can't I get over my partner's affair? *You're not just dealing with infidelity in this relationship but unresolved feelings from a previous one, too.*

47.

I discovered that my husband of 16 years had an inappropriate friendship with a woman in our village. Then six weeks ago he confessed that he had slept with her once in a hotel near her work. (He didn't want me to find out at a later date from someone else.) I have read *How Can I Ever Trust You Again?* which has been really helpful, and my husband has also read it and we have discussed it together. We have also gone to couples counselling as well. We are communicating much better and my husband has been able to express his feelings and emotions, which he has always found difficult. We want to stay together and my husband is doing everything he can to help me recover from this shocking discovery. However, I am still not sleeping or eating very well.

We have become much closer again as a couple but one of my biggest problems is that the OW lives in our small village and I have to pass her house every day and possibly bump into her, which is very difficult because I feel so angry. My husband wants to leave the village as soon as possible but I have always been very happy here until now. What shall I do?

Andrew writes:

First of all, congratulations on the progress that you and your husband have made. I hope the counselling helps with the sleeping and eating issues too.

So what should you do about the OW? Leaving your village sounds drastic – and I've had clients who do move – but I think you should try some other strategies. Let's start with your anger towards this woman. I'd like you to write a letter to her – which you won't post – and tell her everything that you're angry about. Make certain you don't leave anything out! I hope it will be cathartic but more importantly, I want you to go back over it (probably a few days later). Look at where the anger belongs. It could be that some of the anger belongs with your husband. It could be that you're angry with yourself – for example, for not spotting the signs sooner.

Next, I would try some distraction techniques. When you drive or walk past her house, look at the lines in the middle of the road or the birds on the chimney pots opposite – rather than staring at her front door. Alternatively, put on a favourite song on the CD player and sing along. Anything to avoid thinking of her... because basically 'she's not worth it'.

If this does not work, take the opposite approach and think about everything from her point of view. Living in a village, you will probably know a lot about her. My guess is that she is more to be pitied than envied. She must have to be pretty desperate to think a fling with a married man would bring her much happiness! I bet her life is actually rather sad. You might even feel sorry for her (which would probably make her livid because nobody wants to be pitied!).

Finally, I would think through how you'll react when you do finally bump into her. Better to have your plans pre-worked out, rather than be ambushed. Personally, I would go for dignified silence, totally ignoring her or a curt nod (like you might with any distant acquaintance). Remember, she will probably be more mortified than you.

Later, when you're further down the recovery path, look at the issue of forgiveness – for your husband, yourself and even her. I always think of forgiveness as a gift to yourself because it helps you move on (and it's a lot cheaper than moving house)!

Why can't I get over my partner's affair? *You need to find different ways of coping with reminders of your partner's infidelity.*

48. Seven years ago, when I was eight months pregnant, I discovered my husband was cheating on me. I was suspicious because he was so uninterested in me and only barely interested in the pregnancy. I put a tracking programme on our computer. It took screenshots of when he sent emails or used messaging programmes and I discovered a great deal of pornographic use and other women that he was having one-night or several-night stands with.

For five years our relationship was a struggle. He had some counselling, admitted he had always been an unfaithful partner in previous relationships and had always used porn in place of intimacy. There were other discoveries of new women he was plotting to be with, and more discoveries of porn after the initial shocks when I was pregnant, but gradually he seems to have changed and for the past two years has made real efforts to repair our relationship.

I do not believe he is cheating any more and he has moved on from the pornography, again to the best of my knowledge. He has changed his circle of friends, no longer goes out with the boys, and we have many couple friends. He is very focused on family and church.

But I am miserable. All day long I have flashes of things I read, saw, pictures of the other women he cheated with, things that are both real and what I am only imagining. I hate myself, I hate how I look; I am so disgusted with myself, I don't even look in the mirror any more except to quickly check my appearance. We have only had sex maybe three times in the last year. He is trying, but I'm completely uninterested. I don't even want him to see me naked, let alone touch me.

All the women he was with or watched are different from me. I am short, overweight, with small breasts. He apparently has a real attraction to very large-breasted, thinner women.

I know you are thinking, well he picked you to marry so he must like you, but here's the thing: I was the pursuer, I was the chaser early on in our relationship. I got pregnant too soon, unplanned, and now I think he is settling for me, and that just makes me feel repulsive.

During fights or break-ups in the past, he has said he wasn't attracted to me, we have always had a less than normal sex life, and all that combined with his cheating and porn use with women that look nothing like me has left me feeling so hideous. I don't even want to leave the house if I don't have to.

He is trying to fix things, telling me he does want me, that he thinks I am beautiful, but I can't ever believe that. I used to wear lingerie and worry about being sexy or flirting with him, but after all this, I can't even think of putting on that stuff. It would feel so fake. When I wore it before and acted that way, it was because I believed he wanted me, then I found all the other women, saw what they looked like and realised what a fool I was. I feel embarrassed and humiliated that I actually thought a little lace and lipstick would make me attractive – what a moron. It makes me hate myself for being so stupid.

I don't even feel like a woman, just a blob. I'm a mum and housewife, but in terms of gender, I'm a nothing.

I know I can't go back to believing I had any appeal or value as a woman or sexual partner – it's like going back to believing in Santa Claus once you know the truth – but is there some way you can help me at least get to a stage where I can tolerate fulfilling his sexual needs in some way?

Andrew writes:

I hope you manage better than just 'tolerate fulfilling his sexual needs' and instead will actually enjoy sex together, have a happy marriage and, if I'm really shooting for the moon and the stars, to like yourself (just a little bit).

So where do I start? Let's go with the positives. You're going to think I mean that your husband has turned his life round. Sure that's good but the REAL positive is that you're no longer going to believe in Santa Claus! By that I take it, you're not going to think lipstick and lingerie is going to fix this problem or a hundred and one other magical solutions to help you feel better. I know it's really tough to stop believing in Santa but it does at least mean that you can roll up your sleeves and get on with it – rather than waiting for a man in a red coat to arrive and make everything better.

In a strange way, you've been asking your husband to rescue you. I call it outsourcing your self-esteem or welfare to someone else and expecting him to make you like yourself and your body.

- How can he possibly counter-attack a multimillion beauty and fashion business aimed at making women hate themselves and buy their products?

- You're also asking him to sort out the unfortunate influence of a whole line of other people who pulled you down long before he showed up. For example, your mother (who probably had poor body image too and passed her inner critical voice on to you), the girls at school who were cruel, and earlier boy friends who cheated or preferred your friend. Guess what? I doubt your dad made you feel very wanted either.

- I know this is really tough but we all have to take responsibility for our own self-esteem or we're constantly pulled down by a glance from a stranger in a shop (or at least what we THINK they are thinking) or some bad behaviour from our partner (which is normally about their unhappiness and messed-up childhood rather than us).

- He'd also need the training of a counsellor to be able to hear your pain (without getting defensive, full of shame or angry and therefore pushing you away when you need him the most).

I also think you're asking things of yourself that are above your pay scale. For example, asking yourself to combat a multimillion porn industry that is dedicated to making men feel dissatisfied with their love lives. (Porn sites also know how to get into the dark corners of men's sexuality and create desires most had never even considered.) I hope it will also help if I explain that men and women view porn entirely differently. Women have been trained to compare their bodies with other women (hence all the magazines with arrows pointing at wobbly bits of famous women's bodies). Men just use porn as escapism to switch off and de-stress from work – it only has a passing reference to their true sexuality, tastes or desires. The average man honestly doesn't realise (or understand) how women think it is a critique on them. In the same way, you have to take responsibility for your own self-esteem, your husband has to take responsibility for turning himself on – rather than outsourcing to porn or expecting you to magically get him in the mood and combat being tired from work or cranky because the kids have wound him up.

Fortunately, there are lots of good books to help with self-esteem and to begin to repair the damage to your sex life from your husband's porn use and affairs. (I list some of mine in the back of the book.) However, returning to Santa Claus, I don't believe my books will save you either. You will probably need counselling too. However, they can be a building block to help you make the changes – and that ultimately will make you feel a whole lot better.

Why can't I get over my partner's affair? *You have to take responsibility for your own recovery rather than waiting for your partner to make you feel better.*

49. I discovered that my husband had been having an affair with a work colleague for six months while I was temporarily posted to another part of the country. I was totally devastated – we have been married for 20 years and have always both set the greatest store by fidelity. We had also had an extraordinarily close marriage, so the shock was even more profound. After I found out via an anonymous letter (and thank goodness for that letter writer), I confronted him and we then descended into hell for five months as he repeatedly told me that he could not live without her – but he never made any serious attempts to leave the family home. He said so many terrible things to me – that he couldn't live without looking at her beautiful face each day; that she was the love of his life; he could not face 'wasting' the rest of his life with me; that he wished he had had his children with her, and not me.

I did not recognise the man my husband had become – he was monstrous and unspeakably cruel verbally. But despite his awful behaviour, I sensed that to throw him out would be a serious mistake. He then left their mutual workplace to move to another job within the same company and has subsequently realised that he was in a state of limerence during the affair.

He is totally mortified and has worked relentlessly hard since to persuade me of his love, his horror at what he has done and his profound regret. Our situation has not been helped by the fact that the OW has pursued him constantly to the extent that he has had to report it to the police, so persistent did it become.

I know that he is genuinely and completely distraught now about his behaviour, Andrew, and we have worked hard to overcome our mutual pain – counselling, reading your books, endless talking. But ten months after he ended it with her I am still in agony. I simply can't get over the hurt of being told by him during those awful months that he couldn't wait to marry her; that he had never known love like it; that she was everything I am not.

They looked at property together and even visited potential schools for our children and hers – his betrayal was total. He is now bitterly ashamed but despite that I feel as if I am going mad with the pain of it all, and receiving letters from the OW with copies of his intimate and very loving emails to her has been a further agony – not helped by the fact that within those same emails he is horribly disloyal about me. He is desperate for our marriage to continue and I love him with all my heart, but I struggle on a daily basis with forgiveness and we have many rows about it, usually caused by my inability to cope with my pain.

In many senses our marriage has never been better – I had become complacent both sexually and in terms of our emotional intimacy – and we have both had a horrible wake-up call, but I simply can't imagine being able to ever forget the extent and depth of his betrayal. It does not help that the OW is stunningly beautiful and younger than me and has repeatedly mocked me for my physical and other shortcomings in texts and emails.

How do I learn to focus on rebuilding our marriage and banish the memories of his cruelty to me and all that they did and planned together?

Andrew writes:

The more emails I receive, the more I think there is another kind of an affair: Extreme Infidelity. And your experience certainly fits the bill:

husband besotted and completely possessed with limerence and having to report the OW to the police. Horrible. Completely horrible. Under the circumstances, ten months is a blink of the eye and I wonder if you're giving the true date for the nightmare ending (because there is a difference between him calling off the affair and her stopping harassing you). If you count from when you could breath easier, my guess is that we're talking only a few months, so no wonder your body is still on high alert.

How do you move forward? Let me start with some reassurance that you will get over this. However, it will take time, support from your husband and learning some coping mechanisms. If we were working together, I'd like to help you separate fantasy from reality. Because affairs are built on air and dreams, they need constantly to be underpinned with wild promises to make the relationship feel real. So the language is blown up out of all proportion because words are all they have. (Whereas he has solid actions to support his feelings for you.) As all the talk about the future is just castles in the air, to make it seem real the 'lovers' go and look at property and – I admit, an unusual twist – schools for the children.

From your point of view, their plans make their 'love' seem too real. However, to me, it sounds pathetic, desperate and proof that their affair was empty and built on fantasy. Now you might not agree with my take on events, but you can see how it is possible to take the facts presented in their emails, and from your detective work, and build two completely different stories. One drives you mad. The second makes them sound pitiful.

When you're down and depressed, think what you'd really like – my guess is some reassurance, a cuddle and to be told 'I love you'. Instead of letting your fears and pain build up into a tsunami of hurt, try reporting your feelings: 'I'm feeling overwhelmed today' and ask for what you need. Perhaps to talk about some piece of the jigsaw and get clarity or for a little bit of TLC. If you approach everything calmly, your husband is less likely to feel defensive and respond in a helpful rather than destructive way (which gets the two of you fighting again).

I would also like you to keep a diary or blog, where you can write down all your pain and thoughts. They are always better out of your head than turning over and over. Once down on paper, you can begin to sort out the main themes and discuss these issues with your husband (rather than sharing every little concern and making him feel the situation is hopeless). You will also be able to look back and compare how you're doing now with the past. I think you'll find that slowly but surely your relationship is moving in the right direction and you're feeling significantly better.

Be patient with yourself; you've been through a terrible experience but you're doing OK.

Why can't I get over my partner's affair? *You need to separate the fantasy from the reality of the affair.*

50.
The truth about my husband's behaviour has gradually dripped out. The affair had actually been a fully blown physical affair for SEVEN YEARS, starting when I was pregnant with our first child with a couple of breaks in that time. The OW started stalking me online when my husband didn't leave me, repeatedly phoning me and staying silent on the phone late at night. My husband said some terrible things and always talked about the love of his life (not me) etc. However, I just refused to rise to it (most of the time) and gave him a firm ultimatum for making up his mind. I told him I was willing to try but only if he stopped seeing her altogether and we went to counselling. (Then secretly crying to exhaustion when he went to work.)

We had a couple of false starts where he lied about seeing her (even to the counsellor) but finally, during a last-ditch holiday, he admitted everything that had happened (because I had found out everything when I discovered a secret email account). He became committed to his family and trying to work it out with me. I would say it took about six months for the veil to completely lift for him, helped of course by her actions against me which showed him that perhaps she wasn't the person he thought, although in fact I bear her no malice really as he treated her shockingly too. I feel very sorry for her actually, she may have damaged me enormously but in fact she damaged herself far more.

He is now a different husband. In fact it saddens me that we had the relationship we did for so many years. I buried my head in the sand, I didn't see his unhappiness, I didn't see the awful way he was treating me; I was too wrapped up in the children, we shouldn't actually have got married really. I don't know if we would have stayed together when we were still at university if we had faced our problems then.

Things are good now, though. We have since had another baby, we have a lovely family, my husband is very happy and loving towards me. He finally feels he can talk to me. In a way I think the fact that I stayed has given him some confidence in that he's not worried about talking to me about difficult subjects. He feels sick when he thinks about what his life would have been like now without the children all the time, especially the baby who is now four and would only have ever known a part-time father. We still talk about the affair, but in terms of our relationship not his behaviour. I am not emotional about it now at all; in fact I would say my husband can cry about it far more easily than me.

I have two niggling issues, which is why I am writing again.

The first is that if I look at my life today and stay in the present I could not be happier, he really is a wonderful husband, I am very lucky. But if I think about the whole of our relationship I am sad, I long for the fairytale I thought I had. I have had my dreams shattered and I don't seem to be able to let that go. I see my husband through very realistic glasses now and no longer assume we will be together when we are old. I am in love with my husband but not madly IN love with him – this hurts my husband's feelings – does that make sense?

My second issue is my self-esteem; it is very low, my life is constantly about children, I had post-natal depression for a year after the most recent baby and that lack of joy in my life hangs with me. This in turn makes me sad because I see how many good things I have in life. I've put on a large amount of weight and feel very unattractive and I can't help but feel that gradually over time my husband will fall out of love with me again. I should say though that I do trust him; I just know to my cost that anything is possible.

I have moved on but I want to take that final step to complete happiness. That experience has been a really important lesson for both of us. However, I am wasting time thinking about what could have been and what I would like to look like and how I wish I looked different, and that my life is passing me by. I can't believe it's been four years since everything came out. What do you think?

Andrew writes:

I think you should be immensely proud of yourself. Under the most difficult of circumstances, you've held your family together and come out the other side with a loving relationship. Hurrah! In fact, I want to shout it from the highest hill.

However, there are still doubts and niggles; let's go through those. Firstly, if you keep your mind focused on today you couldn't be happier. I think you've answered your own question here. Ultimately it doesn't matter what might have happened if you'd tried to solve your problems at university – what counts is that you've done it now. Secondly, you worry that you've lost the 'fairytale' love and can no longer believe that you will grow old together. Personally, I think the complete opposite. 'Fairytale' love makes people take their partner for granted; it can also stop them seeing their partner's unhappiness. Fortunately, you can now see clearer and have made changes to sort things out. In addition, you have three key qualities for making a relationship last:

1. *Determination.* It is easy to think 'I'll be better off with somebody else', but without learning you just repeat the same mistakes with someone else. Fortunately, you stuck to your guns, learnt, changed and have reaped the rewards.

2. *Forgiveness.* Humans are made of crooked wood. By this I mean, we try to be perfect but we're complicated and flawed beings – so it is best to aim high but be compassionate when we sometimes fail. (I was particularly impressed that you were able to forgive the OW.)

3. *Realism.* Relationships go through tough times and what counts is how you pull yourself through. Often the bad times make us appreciate and love our partner more (I think this is what has happened with your partner).

However, there are still problems. You love your husband but are not madly IN love with him. So what's going on here? There might be a bit of delayed shock and anger. You've been through so much that you can only truly listen to yourself once the adrenaline has stopped pumping through your body. In which case, perhaps there is a bit of resentment, anger and grieving (for the fairytale) to come out. However, I wonder if you just need to reconnect to each other on a different level – away from words – in the bedroom. My suspicion is that you've been feeling less sexual – very common in the first couple of years after a baby. In addition you write that your 'life is all about my children'. Personally, I think there should be some time for you and your husband to be sensual together too. By which I mean lots of kissing and cuddling – without it necessarily leading to sex – so you can begin to reconnect on a profound level. Some mothers feel that sex is just for their husbands but if you are giving out all day to small children, you need someone to give to you – and sensually. Perhaps start by having a bath together, take your time, soap each other down and wash each other's hair, so every part of your body (not just your genitals) feels good. You can finish at that point, but hopefully some love-making will be just the ticket. Ultimately, I think this will help with your self-esteem.

So why not think about the type of love-making that you'd like, arrange for someone to have the kids, and take some time to reconnect sexually again? OK, you will need to be brave but I think you've learn how to be courageous from all your trials and tribulations over the past four years – use those new skills and reap the benefits.

Why can't I get over my partner's affair? *You need to mourn for the relationship that you thought you had before you can have a new 'eyes open' version.*

50 REASONS WHY YOU CAN'T GET OVER YOUR PARTNER'S AFFAIR

I've recapped the key learning points so that when you're feeling down you can look through the list, find which common sticking point resonates and re-read the relevant advice.

1. It is early days in the recovery process.

2. Recovery is not a straight line.

3. You're trying to control your partner and his or her lover when the only things you can truly control is your own thoughts, reactions and behaviour.

4. You're expecting a full confession but lots of people take months and months to admit to the basic details.

5. You need to get your confidence back and believe that you're worthy of your partner's love.

6. You need to focus on working on yourself rather than waiting for your partner to change.

7. You've had an understandable setback. So go back to basics – like improving communication – and don't let it derail your recovery.

8. You need to face the past rather than run away from it.

9. You're focusing too much on what happened and not enough on why.

10. You're suppressing your anger.

11. You haven't addressed the real reasons for your partner's unfaithfulness and inability to commit.

12. It takes time to negotiate a way forward that's acceptable to both of you.

13. It's still going on.

14. In the rush to resolve your problems, you have been pushing your partner away, which has increased your anxiety and compounded the problem further.

15. You're still deciding which way to jump and that's fine because it is better to make a considered rather than an impulsive decision.

16. You've both stopped talking and listening to each other.

17. You have been so busy criticising his or her behaviour that you have downgraded or overlooked your own contribution to this crisis.

18. Everybody else in the family is involved, pumping up your distress and making it harder to see what's really happening.

19. The longer and more serious the affair, the longer it takes to recover and the better your communication needs to be.

20. You are obsessed with one element of the affair and can't look past it.

21. A fresh discovery has sent you back into shock again.

22. You're still trying to understand the complexity of your partner's behaviour.

23. You need to be assertive rather than alternate between being passive and domineering.

24. There are issues in your sex life that still need to be addressed.

25. You are trying to fight natural and necessary feelings rather than accepting and learning from them.

26. You need to understand the link between thoughts and feelings.

27. It's brought up issues from your childhood which need to be faced.

28. You have been so focused on your partner that you have neglected your own needs.

29. You need to focus more on getting through today rather than worrying about an unknowable future.

30. You need to build yourself up and feel strong enough to decide your next move.

31. You need to give your partner time and space to sort through his or her feelings rather than expect him or her to fit into your time-table for moving forward.

32. You have been really hurt and it will take time to recover.

33. You keep going round and round the same loop.

34. Looking for revenge keeps you bound to the past and stops you making a better future.

35. You need to write down your fears rather than letting them go round and round in your head.

36. You have been focusing on finding quick fixes, which make everything worse rather than better.

37. You need to find compassion for your partner, yourself and even the affair partner.

38. You're focusing on how life *should* be rather than how dealing with the reality of how it *is*.

39. You're setting an arbitrary test for your partner about how committed he or she is to your relationship and setting both your partner and yourself up for failure.

40. It's OK to be in limbo at the moment – especially if you're still learning and growing.

41. Affairs are often made up of many layers of deception – each of which needs to be made sense of and worked through.

42. Your recovery might not feel secure but you're making really good progress.

43. Your partner is suffering from a mental illness and is currently unable to face the enormity of what he or she has done.

44. You need to focus on taking care of yourself at the moment rather than healing your marriage.

45. You need to own up to the depth of the problems between the two of you.

46. You're not just dealing with infidelity in this relationship but unresolved feelings from a previous one too.

47. You need to find different ways of coping with reminders of your partner's infidelity.

48. You have to take responsibility for your own recovery rather than waiting for your partner to make you feel better.

49. You need to separate the fantasy from the reality of the affair.

50. You need to mourn for the relationship that you thought you had before you can have a new 'eyes open' version.

CONCLUSION

In an ideal world, your partner would have made a full and timely confession (rather than continued to lie or hold back important information) and decided whether he or she wanted to be married or not (rather than kept in contact with the affair partner). However, in an ideal world, he or she would have spoken up about his or her unhappiness and avoided the infidelity in the first place. So instead of hankering after how you believe recovery should go, or wishing that your partner's betrayal had been extreme or more understandable, it's better to challenge your expectations.

SEVEN MYTHS ABOUT INFIDELITY THAT MAKE RECOVERY HARDER

The media and our wishful thinking has promoted a set of myths about affairs. In many cases, these myths are so deeply embedded in our culture that you're not really conscious of them. So look at the following and see how many you believe and ask yourself what the impact of believing them might have been.

Your partner will confess everything in one go

When your partner says he or she will do 'anything' to make up for the betrayal, you'd think that would include complete honesty. So when he or she doesn't make a clean breast, you draw one of two obvious conclusions: your partner did not mean it (which reinforces the idea that he or she is a devious stranger) or your partner truly loves the affair partner (and wants to protect him or her). However, the truth is most likely far more complicated. Your partner is in shock. He or she has just realised the full implication of the betrayal (because he or she has minimised the bad behaviour and pretended it won't hurt anyone else) and is full of self-loathing. So he or she can't bear to say 'I brought her to our house' or 'I would meet him at the school gates, so our children know him.' Overwhelmed with shame, your partner imagines if he or she doesn't give these details that they can't 'hurt' you but actually he or she is trying to protect him or herself from facing up to the full extent of the betrayal.

I doubt that you will have much sympathy – quite rightly – but I find that many discovered partners who 'deny, deny, deny' had a childhood that traumatised them in some way. Sometimes one of their parents had an affair or affairs and this caused years of unhappiness and anger. Realising that they have repeated their parents' mistakes, and have subjected their own children to the same behaviour, will deepen the shock and compound the compulsion to withhold. Sometimes one of their parents had mental health or anger issues and anything beyond 'perfect' behaviour from their children caused chaotic or depressive behaviour (or maybe, worse still, it was impossible to predict the triggers). More commonly parents regularly used shame and exclusion to ensure their son or daughter did what they were told. Shame is the most powerful of emotions – because it is the complete opposite of love – and should be used incredibly sparingly on children who are still learning to deal with complex feelings. Their unformed brain will either shut down (as an adult this manifests as walking away, complete denial and acting coldly) or blow all the circuits (hence adult hysterical reactions like threatening suicide, getting angry or floods of tears).

Turn it round: I have yet to meet someone who tells everything on the first asking; sometimes it is because your partner does not think some details are important, but normally the reticence is more about shame or fear of your reaction than his or her feelings for you.

The pain gets a little less every day

I wish with all my heart that this was 100 per cent true but it is only a partial truth. When you're finally out of the trenches and looking back over the journey, it will seem sort of true: recovery is gradual but steady. However in the first weeks, months (and sometimes years) after discovery, the pain comes in fits and starts. Something will remind you of the betrayal. Half of all TV programmes include infidelity and if you throw in lies and deceit that's probably most of them. Celebrities and politicians are always being caught out being unfaithful and it will seem that all your friends and work colleagues have had similar experiences too. Although your partner will be trying to make it up, he or she will be full of despair and do stupid things that set you both back. The affair partner will probably not disappear off the face of the earth. You will discover new aspects of the betrayal and you'll feel thrown back to the first day.

On other occasions, it will be something innocent like traffic delays and a phone out of battery power. Your partner is late home and your heart is racing; the anxiety is overwhelming. It is easy to catastrophise and think, 'I will never get over this' and the 'betrayal was too great' – and that might be the case – but more likely the problem is that you've been profoundly hurt, it takes time to recover and the journey involves going backwards as well as forwards.

Turn it round: You partner is unlikely to stop lying straight away. It takes a while to break old habits – especially if he or she hates conflict – and learn the necessary skills to face rather than avoid difficult situations. So be patient with your partner and yourself, it takes longer than you would wish to get over infidelity – especially with extreme betrayal. What counts is not how quickly you recover but how much you learn and improve your communication.

Your partner needs to break off all contact with the other man or woman

We are back to my ideal world again. I don't want your partner to contact the affair partner. It makes my task tougher. However, I am a realist. It is harder to make a clean break in the age of social media. Smartphones have made our homes more porous. The 'lovers' will have had 'feelings' for each other – although pumped up and unrealistic – and it will take time to grieve for what they had (even if it is really an illusion). Sometimes there are layers of relationship that need to be let go – not just a sexual relationship but an underlying friendship too.

Unfortunately, our society is not good at mourning and does not understand the process. So people often mistake natural parts of grieving – like thinking about the ex and wondering 'What if?' – as signs that they 'should' be together or that they 'can't get over the affair'. That's why an important part of my work is educating: it's OK to grieve and it's an important part of moving on.

Of course, it would be easier if your partner didn't rub salt in the wound by contacting his or her affair partner but it is important to keep a sense of proportion. It is a setback, not the end of your relationship.

Turn it round: Only a minority of affairs have a clean break.

Especially with extreme infidelity, there are often false dawns before contact finally ends. However, I've worked with hundreds of couples where there was still intermittent interaction with the affair partner – or the 'lovers' still worked together – but it did not prevent my clients from saving their marriage (just made it a bit harder). If you are calm about the latest discovery, you will have a more rational discussion, make a better assessment of the damage and be less likely to push your partner into despair (and prompt more emails, texts and clandestine chats with the other man or woman).

What your partner told his or her 'lover' is the truth

One of the problems of so much of our communication being by text, email and online chat is that none of this information disappears. So if you are minded – like most people – to read all the sexy flirting or extravagant promises of undying love, you can 'know' everything about the affair. However, it is important to take what was typed with not a pinch but a whole bucket or maybe even a lorry load of salt! I'm sorry to admit it but men will say practically anything to get into a woman's knickers. While real relationships are built on extended time together and sharing day-to-day reality, affairs are built on snatched time together and escapism. Therefore, fantasy plays a huge part in affairs – almost as much as lying. Perhaps they are interchangeable. Time and again, in my counselling room, when the discovered partner is challenged he will say, 'I knew that's what she (or he) wanted to hear'.

Turn it round: Your partner is just as likely to have lied about his or her feelings to the affair partner as he or she has done to you. Even if your partner did believe that the other man or woman was the 'love of their life', it was probably only true for a passing moment (despite the text being around for eternity).

Your partner will know what he or she wants (and stick to it)

If by force of will, I could make just one of these myths true it would be this one. Nothing causes more pain in my counselling room. So let me try and shine light on what's going on. Firstly, the affair can be the tip of a much larger problem. Your partner is at a crossroads, no longer finding his or her job satisfying, the children are about to leave home or perhaps one of his or her parents has died and that's making life feel empty or meaningless. Your partner had an affair to feel better and although the state of your marriage is part of the problem it's not the whole picture. Under these circumstances, asking should I stay or go is the wrong question (so no wonder trying to answer it is making everything more confused rather than less). Secondly, the worst part of infidelity is that the discovered partner is not only lying to his or her partner (and 'lover') but also to him or herself. For example, 'We won't get caught out' or 'What happens over here has no impact on over there'. If you're in the habit of lying to yourself, how can you possibly know what you want? Finally, shock and trauma – which is par for the course after infidelity is uncovered – does not make for good decision-making.

Turn it round: Your partner might not know his or her mind but you can decide what you want – and try to stick to it. If you are consistent and calm that will help your partner move in that direction, too. If you change your mind from moment to moment, you will pump up the drama and your relationship will descend into a soap opera or even tragedy. Although you can't control your partner's behaviour, you can control your reactions.

We can quickly put this behind us

The myths about affairs reinforce each other. After all, if your partner confesses everything and breaks off all contact with the affair partner, the pain will get less and less and you can put everything behind you (if not quickly, at least in a timely manner). So, just last week I had a Discovered partner in my office saying: 'We've been going over and over this for six months now, shouldn't my husband be ready to move on?' I smiled understandingly and she immediately retracted: 'It's only been six months'. They had been childhood sweethearts and when my client's husband was about 15, his parents had split up for 18 months after his father went off with another woman. Even 30 years later, my client's husband had not forgiven his father for the pain caused to everybody. No wonder these clients couldn't quickly put this behind them.

Turn it round: There are no shortcuts to feeling better. Even divorce does not take away the pain or make the problems caused by infidelity go away. Recovery takes whatever time it takes and that's fine, because it's better to keep working on improving your relationship than pretending everything is OK.

You need closure

I hear this over and over again: 'I want closure.' It sounds like a great idea being able to shut the door on the hurt, rejection, guilt, shame and betrayal, but I wonder if it is actually possible. While most terms – like closure – have their roots in either psychology or religion, we seem to have made this one up because we long for it so much. When my partner died – 18 years ago – I longed for closure, but even though I'm in a second long-term relationship and have written extensively about bereavement, I can still surprise myself by crying about some aspect of my loss. Have I reached closure? On many occasions, I've thought I had, but actually I'm more and more convinced that it's an illusion.

Turn it round: Borrowing a term from Christianity, I think of transcending pain rather than closure. You can achieve this goal by learning, growing and creating a better relationship. Although you will never forget what happened, you can value the lessons that the experience has taught you. In this way, you transcend the pain.

SEVEN COMMON TRAPS ON THE ROAD TO RECOVERY

I've been dealing with infidelity for 30 years and since writing my book on affairs, I've counselled hundreds of couples who have got stuck in the recovery process, and heard from people in despair from the four corners of the earth. Although the circumstances are always different, people fall into the same seven traps.

Making assumptions

One of the problems of long-established couples is that they *think* they know their partners so well that they *know* what they are thinking or can deduce why they did something. On lots of occasions, the conclusions are right (or close enough not to matter). However, infidelity throws everything upside down. While in the past your assumptions were fairly benign – your partner was distracted because he or she was busy at work, because he or she couldn't possibly be having an affair – now they are intensely negative. Your partner didn't return your call not because there was rush on at work but because he or she does not make you a priority.

Turn it round: Rather than assuming, I would rather you asked: Why didn't you call back? If you think you know the answer, check it out: You were distracted yesterday, were you thinking of her? You might be right but it could be for an innocent reason, so find out before you have a row (rather than afterwards when you have both calmed down). It might seem time-consuming but you will be restoring the 'grand dialogue' of your marriage and discovering new things about each other.

Using the affair to always be in the right

Every couple has disagreements but after an affair these become not about the issue at hand – for example, who should have the car tonight – but about the affair. Instead of discussing the merits of each person's case, your partner accuses you of being controlling and you're angry because this is another example of his or her selfishness. Worse still, you have a trump card: the affair. By laying it down, you can 'win' any argument, and lots of unfaithful partners end up muttering under their breath: 'It doesn't matter what I say, I'll always be in the wrong.' Not only does this stop good communication and make negotiation (one of the key elements of assertiveness) harder but it makes both you and your partner feel hopeless (because even a minor pinch can cause an almighty crunch).

Turn it round: If you feel yourself tempted to bring up the affair – even if in your mind there is a direct link between the matter in hand and the infidelity – please resist the temptation. While it is perfectly possible that you will be able to sort out the pinch (for example, whose turn it is to have the car), I doubt that linking this argument to the affair will produce a breakthrough in your recovery. I know your partner has committed a terrible sin – infidelity often brings up this sort of biblical language – but acting self-righteous (by which I mean having an exaggerated idea of your own virtue) is deeply unattractive and previous generations considered it a sin too. In most cases, the desire to keep bringing up the affair is either a sign that there is something that you need to discuss calmly with your partner or that you need a bit of TLC and reassurance. In both cases, it is better to ask for what you need rather than escalate an argument in the distant hope of getting some relief.

Looking for magic solutions

This is a trap which your partner fell into. His or her life doesn't make sense any more, but instead of doing the hard work of finding out why or trying to turn raound your marriage, he or she found an instant solution: flirting with someone, going on a hook-up site, and you know the rest. Human beings like easy and quick solutions. Therefore I'm not surprised that you are pinning all your hopes on a holiday (to make a fresh start), or getting divorced and remarried to your partner (to surgically remove the old relationship) or getting the affair partner out of your lives (so your partner can concentrate on the marriage). I could go on because over the past 30 years, I've heard hundreds and hundreds. Of course each of these changes could be a part your recovery – perhaps a key part – but it's not going to be the silver bullet. However, while you are 'persuading' (or more likely emotionally blackmailing) your partner to follow your plan, you are not listening to him or her and setting yourself up for a major setback when the magical solution does not transform your relationship.

Turn it round: I know you're in pain and want to feel better, but there are no magic shortcuts. The pain will shrink down to manageable proportions if you focus on living in the moment. I have a question for when you're stressed and overwhelmed: Can I cope with now? (By which I mean today, tomorrow and the day after.) The answer is generally yes. It's when you start worrying about the months ahead (forthcoming holidays, etc) and the rest of your life that the pain becomes unbearable. Alternatively, you could be living in the past and feeling nostalgic for your old relationship; gently try and bring your attention back to today and forging a new, better version.

Needing to know everything

On one hand, hearing the story of the affair and no longer being the only person in the dark is part of the healing process. On the other hand, it is easy to tip into torturing yourself and punishing your partner. It also encourages obsessive detective work, hyper-vigilance and finding distressing information or images that get burnt on to the back of your brain. In the meantime, the longer after the affair finished, the more likely your partner is to forget details of what happened or simply refuse to go through everything again. At this point, you are blocked and angry because it seems your partner is preventing your healing and how can you believe his or her protestations of love if he or she won't do this one simple thing for you?

Turn it round: Start by questioning if knowing everything is really so important – especially if your partner can't explain why he or she was unfaithful, the explanations don't make sense or are simply inadequate. You could have tipped over into magical thinking – 'If I know everything, I can make sense of the affair and I will feel better' – or maybe you will never understand (because men and women often view the world differently). Therefore, I suggest trying different types of questions. Rather than asking your partner to compare you to the affair partner or remember the number of times he or she went to a particular hotel, switch to deeper and more psychologically penetrating questions. For example, What did the affair mean to you? What parts of yourself could you not express with me? What did you feel that you couldn't tell me? and What do you value about me today? I hope you can see how these will prompt less defensive answers and more revealing discussions.

You broke it, so you fix it

I have a lot of sympathy for this position. It's really helpful if your partner does try to make things better, and helping your recovery is an important part of atoning for his or her betrayal. However, 'you broke it, so you *must* fix it' causes all sorts of problems. We're back to the ideal world again because this concept pre-supposes that your partner has enough emotional insight to properly explain why he or she was unfaithful, has enough emotional intelligence to avoid the obvious own goals during recovery and good enough communication skills to resolve any setbacks. Sadly, if your partner possessed all these qualities, I doubt you would be in this mess and you certainly wouldn't be so stuck that you're reading this book!

Turn it round: Ultimately, the person best placed to sort out your pain is YOU. So how are you going to achieve that? Firstly, you can work on your self-knowledge, your emotional intelligence and your communication skills. (See the suggested reading at the back of the book.) Secondly, you can work on balancing your own life. Let me try and explain. Infidelity hurts even more when your partner has been your best friend, companion, confident, life coach, financial provider, etc. all rolled into one – because his or her infidelity is a stark demonstration of your vulnerability. So look at spreading the load and filling in the gaps so that whatever happens next you will feel stronger. For example, finding more friends or re-training. Thirdly, think about forgiveness. We imagine that our partner has to earn forgiveness but actually giving it is a gift to yourself because forgiveness allows you to move on and feel better.

Believing the affair is alive and well

I know it is easy to think that if your partner and the other woman or man are still in contact the affair is alive and well. So let me tell you about a couple that I counselled. We met for the first time a couple of days after the husband decided to end his affair (after six months of indecision). He described himself as 'sort of committed' to working on his marriage. I was pleased that he was honest about his concerns as this gave me an opportunity to talk about grieving and this allowed the couple to openly discuss it when the husband was withdrawn. However, over the following weeks, he met up with his affair partner for a drink on a Friday night after work (but took several days to tell his wife) and the OW ambushed him outside his house when he came back home late (but he woke up his wife and told her). I was fascinated to discover that the 'ambush' had been helpful rather than harmful to recovery. He explained: 'We went over the same old things again and I thought, "What did I ever see in this woman"' and "How could I have come so close to losing everything?"' I had a picture of a chicken that had its head chopped off but was still running round the farmyard. To a casual observer, a headless chicken looks alive but it's about to fall to the ground lifeless. So turning to your partner, does his or her contact suggest that the affair is alive and well or in its death throes?

Turn it round: Affairs bring out a lot of black-and-white thinking: 'guilty' and 'innocent', 'right' and 'wrong', 'good' or 'evil', and 'alive' or 'dead'. However, life is always more complicated and instead of jumping to conclusions, talk to your partner, listen without interruption (or telling him what he or she is thinking), ask for clarification and make an informed decision. You might not to be able to reach a definitive conclusion but 'watch and wait' is always better than false certainty.

Catastrophising

Like the myths about affairs, the traps while recovering interlock and reinforce each other. If you make assumptions, you are likely to believe that the affair is alive and well. When magical thinking fails to provide the instant solution or your partner refuses to discuss again some part of the affair, you are full of despair. If you're always right and expect your partner to fix things (while he or she has tried but is out of ideas), then your partner will be full of despair. At this point, you will both be catastrophising – by which I mean painting your relationship in the worst possible light, your coping skills as zero and the pain as never-ending. No wonder you want to throw in the towel.

Turn it round: When you reach this point, write down all of your thinking or type it into your phone. Thoughts are better on paper or the screen than in your head, because there you can challenge them. Take out all the absolute words like 'never' and 'always' and 'should' and 'must'. Next, go back through the list and take out all the exaggerations and turn statements into questions. For example: 'I can't get over this pain' into: 'How can I get over my pain?' Finally, cross out anything that is actually untrue. When I do this exercise with clients, they often go from ten on the anxiety scale to six. At this point, they have stopped catastrophising and are ready to think more clearly.

THE NUMBER-ONE SKILL FOR TURNING YOUR RELATIONSHIP AROUND

My top tip will not come as a surprise if you've read the first part of this book or my other books because good communication – not only over big things but day-to-day issues – is at the heart of all my work. Good communication is also the best way to not only recover but lay down foundations for a better relationship (either with your partner or with someone else). So let me go into the details. There are four types of communication that undermine relationships and while none of them are too bad in the short-term, over time, they will build a wedge between you and your partner. Fortunately, there is a fifth alternative, which I will outline too.

Being passive

Definition: *My needs, wants and beliefs are of little importance and yours are of supreme importance.*

These are people pleasers who want to make others happy or believe that if they fulfil their partner's needs they will reciprocate. Unfortunately, they are often disappointed (because if they don't say anything how will their partner know) and they often end up resentful and angry. Alternatively, they will minimise and rationalise away their upset: 'It doesn't matter' or 'Anything for a quiet life.' However, we cannot pick and choose which feelings we switch off, pretty soon we're switching off the nice ones too and saying, 'I love you but I'm not in love with you' or sinking into depression.

Being domineering

Definition: *My needs, wants and beliefs are of supreme importance and yours are of lesser importance.*

Sometimes this form of communication is called aggressive but it's perfectly possible to get your own way without shouting or losing your temper. Sometimes these people will manipulate behind the scenes, so their partner thinks something was their idea. They can also play the martyr and guilt their partner into fulfilling their needs. I know these people sound horrible but generally they're perfectly reasonable and normal. They just believe their way is right (children should go to bed at eight) and therefore their beliefs should trump their partner (who does not properly understand the situation or is simply wrong).

Using domain specific communication

Definition: *I make the decisions in some areas (where my needs, wants and beliefs are of supreme importance) and you make the decisions in other areas (where my needs, wants and beliefs are of secondary importance).*

Many couples exist happily with this style for years. The most common example would be a traditional marriage where she is in charge of the home and children and he controls money and everything outside the house. With all things considered, the power balances up and these couples would say 'we make a good team'. However, changed circumstances – like children leaving home or losing a job – can throw everything off kilter.

Swinging between passive and domineering

Definition: *I will generally downgrade my needs, wants and beliefs to accommodate yours, but sometimes I become so fed up or angry that I declare my wishes of supreme importance and ignore yours.*

This is what happens in affairs when a partner who is generally a people pleaser (passive) gets so fed up or low that he or she feels that they deserve or have to put their needs first (domineering). Outside infidelity, a predominately passive person will suddenly snap and demand things are done his or her way (and their shocked partner quickly backs down), will unilaterally make a decision (and come home driving an expensive sports car), or go behind their partner's back (and let the children stay up till midnight if they 'promise' not to tell).

Being assertive

Definition: *My needs, wants and beliefs are important and so are yours.*

This is the alternative fifth way of communicating. With both partner's having equal rights, what happens when there is a clash? I describe assertiveness as 'I can ask, you can say no and we can negotiate.' The negotiation takes time but should lead to a compromise (a third option that is acceptable to both parties), a trade (I will do this for you, if you do that for me) or conceding (because after much discussion I accept you have a better case but I feel properly heard and therefore withdraw my request). It seems straightforward, but we find it difficult to ask (because we are frightened of being rejected or trained as children not to be 'pushy') and hard to say no (because we are frightened our partner will be upset and maybe not like us), and negotiation is difficult too (because we're not taught it at school and when we were children our parents probably used one of the other four styles). However, learning to be assertive is the foundation for a new and better marriage. There is more advice on this topic in my other books – in particular *Wake Up and Change Your Life: How to survive a crisis and be stronger, wiser and happier.*

WHAT IF YOU STILL CAN'T GET OVER YOUR PARTNER'S AFFAIR?

There are bound to be times when you will despair. Our culture is very down on people who still love their partner and want to save their marriage despite infidelity. I had a glimpse of the pressure that you might be under when I was publicising my book *My Husband Doesn't Love Me and He's Texting Someone Else* – note I was just talking about 'texting' and not necessarily an emotional or physical affair (although it can easily lead to this dark place). The hosts of the TV and radio shows were united that at the first sign of any 'cheating' it should be 'throw him out' or 'leave her'. If I asked, 'What if the person still loved their partner' or they were worried about the 'impact on the kids', I was told 'once a cheater, always a cheater' or they should have more 'self-respect' and 'find someone that deserves them'. Alternatively, the audience simply turned on me with a fervour which I could only describe as 'burn the witch'. While previous generations considered divorce the great taboo, we have gone 180 degrees and made staying and working on your relationship the great unmentionable (and therefore hard to discuss with your friends and get continuing support from them). I hope this book has made you feel less alone.

So what should you do if you're feeling down? I hope you will be compassionate to yourself. You have chosen a difficult path but one that is ultimately much more rewarding. Learning to communicate better with your partner is always beneficial – either to repair your relationship or to cooperate better as co-parents if that is not possible. I've also found that people who tried to save their marriage make a better recovery after divorce than those who simply walked away. I had a friend whose wife died and when he felt strong enough to go on a dating site, who do you think he met? Lots of women whose partners had cheated and were looking for someone who 'deserved' them. He found them suspicious, unable to trust and jealous. In other words, they had 'moved on' but were still carrying all the baggage from their marriage. It is always better to try and work through these feelings with the person concerned than in your next relationship or with casual dates! So trust me, none of this work on yourself and your communication skills is going to be wasted. You are doing remarkably well; it might only be survival at the moment but that's a good start. Be patient with yourself, and your partner, and the panic, anxiety and pain will subside to a more manageable level. The best decisions about your future are made when you've reached a calmer place and the initial crisis or trigger point for a fresh crisis has passed.

As well as compassion and patience, I have one more piece of advice: keep talking. It will take some of the burden off your shoulders and help you to understand your partner's different burden. It will also help to keep hope alive for a better future. And on that note, let me finish with another letter.

> *Today I'm OK, but definitely not fully recovered. The affair, for my partner, ended with my discovery but it was, for me, the beginning of the most traumatic period I have ever lived through.*
>
> *The huge problem is triggers, the unexpected ones that can be set off by the most far-fetched associations. This is just an example, but my husband's OW was Brazilian. When I see someone in the street wearing a T-shirt with the Brazilian flag on it, I do a double take and all the memories come*

flooding back. The emotion is not as intense as it was, but it's still there. I avoid all things to do with Brazil, language, films, music. I won't allow any images or souvenirs of this country in my house.

All memories of the past are also tagged with a 'before' or 'after' label. Shared holidays between the beginning of the affair and discovery have become contaminated. You look at holiday photos and you think 'How could you (partner) have pretended you were happy with me when you were just thinking of her?'

This is what's most difficult during recovery. You almost wish that you could be lobotomised and have the whole affair cut out of your brain!!!

The following things would have helped me immensely during these months after discovery:

- *The truth, the whole truth and nothing but the truth. No more lies were told, but answers to questions and information about the affair were given in a 'drip, drip' fashion. It's not a kinder way to be honest.*

- *Daily apologies, written, spoken. Not 'I regret...' but 'I'm truly sorry...'*

- *Couples counselling straight away. I've always communicated easily with my spouse, but in the case of discovered infidelity, whatever happens, communication becomes either accusatory, defensive and even hysterical.*

- *An acknowledgement of my immense suffering on the part of the medical profession. I know I suffered from PTAS (Post-traumatic Affair Syndrome) but I was given antidepressants and told to practise self-control.*

- *A proper end to the affair with the OW. A phone call,*

with me by my partner's side, telling this woman that she must now move out of our lives. I wrote emails, he wrote emails, but nothing was done together. I think no one realises how the affair partner can continue to live on in the couple's lives long after the end of an affair. This has been the major problem for us in terms of intimacy.

The following things have helped me on the road to recovery (I'm still on it!):

- *Physical activity. In my case it's gardening. Weed pulling is quite cathartic!*

- *Getting more involved in my work (not at all easy as I don't have much job-satisfaction).*

- *Looking at the greater picture, the problems of our planet, reading the thoughts of those who rose, or rise, above the fray (Dalai Lama, Nelson Mandela, etc).*

- *Loving my children more. They too need to be cherished and helped. One of my children definitely suffered through what was happening to her parents.*

- *Educating my partner through books about affairs and what they do to families. My husband was not aware of so many things before reading the articles and books I gave him. His awareness has helped me tremendously.*

- *Writing down things in a diary for my eyes only.*

- *Time.*

Finally, the expressions 'to break one's heart' or 'to have one's heart broken' have taken on a completely new meaning for me. I literally felt that this vital pump in my chest was going to explode with all the pain that it was channelling. However, it is recovering, but needs a lot of time to function fully again.

All that is left is to thank this reader of my blog for sharing her journey and wish you all the best in your recovery. Remember, you CAN get over your partner's affair.

Andrew G. Marshall
www.andrewgmarshall.com

FURTHER READING

How Can I Ever Trust You Again?

If you haven't read the classic book on the seven stages of recovering from infidelity, it will help make sense of your feelings and reassure that they are normal and understandable. There's also my detailed plan on how to come out of this crisis with a stronger and better marriage. Each chapter ends with a short section written for the partner who has been unfaithful and many couples find these prompt constructive conversations on how to move forward. The book also includes:

- The eight types of affairs and how understanding your partner's is key to rescuing your relationship.

- How to stop your imagination running wild and your brain going into meltdown.

- How the person who had the affair can help their partner recover.

- What derails recovery and how to get your marriage on track again.

Wake Up and Change Your Life

Discovering that your partner has had an affair doesn't just trigger a crisis in your relationship but in your own confidence, self-worth, and can even call into question your whole identity. This book explains how his or her infidelity can re-activate unresolved problems from your past, how to keep calm in the face of enormous provocation and how to find meaning in your life again. It also includes:

- Improving your communication (one of the key elements for turning round your relationship).

- Coping with anxiety and depression.

- The importance of boundaries for yourself and your relationship.

- Nine simple maxims to transform your life.

What Is Love?

Love is one of the most powerful forces in our lives but it is also one of the most misunderstood. This book combines some of the greats minds who have written about love from across the ages with 50 letters from people just like you. One of the great problems of infidelity is that you can feel very alone and this book reveals other people's dilemmas and my advice for moving forward. Many of my clients, dealing with infidelity, read this book with their

partner because it prompts useful discussions about love and relationships without getting caught in the same old loops. Sections include:

- The spark went out.

- Being torn between a partner and a lover.

- Restoring love after an affair.

- Making amends.

My Husband Doesn't Love Me and He's Texting Someone Else

Men fall out of love for different reasons to women and this book will explain the three things every woman needs to know to protect her relationship. It is also full of practical techniques for coming back from the brink – like assertiveness – and advice on diagnosing whether your husband is depressed (plus what to do if he is). In the second half of the book, I tackle what to do if you suspect or know the affair is still continuing:

- The six types of other woman, from 'a spark' to 'the love of his life'.

- Tailored strategies for dealing with each type.

- Five worst and best reactions after uncovering what's really going on.

- How to keep calm even when provoked.

- How to combat the poison that she's slipping into your relationship.

- When to keep fighting and when to make a tactical withdrawal.

My Wife Doesn't Love Me Any More

If your life is in turmoil because your wife has just told you that she doesn't love you and your marriage is over, this book will bring a bit of sanity into your world. In my experience, more relationships end at this point not because women are determined to leave but because men panic and end up pushing their wife even further away. In this book, I explain how to keep calm and listen, really listen rather than argue or trying to find a magic fix. I also cover:

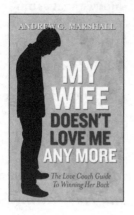

- How to figure out why she's fallen out of love.

- Five things you think will save your relationship but should absolutely avoid.

- What her words and actions really mean and how to use them to win her back.

- What to do to instantly improve the atmosphere at home.

- How to prevent past mistakes from undermining your attempts to build a better future.

- Five pick-me-up tips for when you're down and need to keep focused.

- When it's time to admit it's over and what factors indicate you should still fight on.

I Love You But You Always Put Me Last

One of the key reasons why couples become estranged is that they put so much energy into raising their kids that they neglect their marriage. However, you don't need to choose between a happy marriage and happy children; you can have them both. I explain how to parent as a team and raise an emotionally healthy family. Packed with tips, advice and compelling examples, this book will equip you to turn your marriage round. I explain how to:

- Ask for the support you need.

- Overcome differences in parenting styles and find acceptable compromises.

- Share household responsibilities effectively.

- Define what your children truly need from you.

- Rekindle your passion for each other and keep it alive.

- Avoid the pitfalls of raising 'red-carpet kids' and give your children a strong foundation for the future.

I Love You But I'm Not In Love With You

Over 100,000 copies sold worldwide. This book will help you get to the roots of why the affair happened, why seemingly loving partners detach and how that can let someone else into your relationship. There is more information about limerence and how to speak your partner's love language. Also includes:

- How to argue productively and address the core of the issue.

- Employ the trigger words for more effective communication.

- Find a balance between being fulfilled as an individual and being one half of a couple.

- Create new bonds instead of searching for old ones.

Learn to Love Yourself Enough

If you're trying to recover from your partner's affair, it's easy to think everything would be better if only my partner would... (fill in the blank). However, that closes off one of the most powerful and effective ways forward: working on yourself. After all, if you're calmer and in a better place, you will communicate better and the dynamics of your whole relationship will change. In this book, I will help you step back, get to know yourself better and rebuild your shattered self-confidence. It covers how to:

- Examine your relationship with your parents: Discover the six types of child-parent relationships and how to accept the legacy of your past.

- Find forgiveness: Debunk the two myths about forgiveness and discover what can be gained from negative experiences.

- Don't let other people put you down: Recognise the five phases of projection and how understanding our own projections leads to better and happy relationships.

- Re-program your inner voice: Identify the three kinds of negative thinking that work together to undermine self-confidence and whether they are based on fact or just opinion.

- Set realistic goals: Learn how perfectionism undermines self-esteem.

- Re-balance yourself: Understand that problems lurk in the extremes and why the middle way is the most successful way.

- Conquer fears and setbacks: Overcome the day-to-day problems that life and other people throw at you.

Have the Sex You Want

If your sex life has not recovered from your partner's affair or is more about going through the motions than building connection, this book is for you. It will help you challenge the myths about sex that are stopping passionate love-making, break down the bad habits that have accumulated over your years together and re-build your sex life into something sensual and more plentiful. At the core is a ten-week proven plan for restoring

intimacy which builds slowly until you have the sex you've always wanted. I also show how to:

- Talk about sex with your partner without getting defensive.

- Deal with different levels of desire.

- Understand the three types of making love and how they can rekindle desire.

- Repair the damage from an affair by reconnecting again in the bedroom.

ABOUT THE AUTHOR

Andrew G. Marshall is a marital therapist with 30 years' experience. He trained with RELATE (the UK's leading couple counselling charity) but now leads a team in private practice in London and Sussex offering the Marshall Method. He is also the author of 16 other books on relationships and contributes to *The Mail on Sunday*, *Sunday Telegraph*, *The Times* and women's magazines around the world. To date, his work has been translated into over 20 different languages. To receive regular updates about Andrew's books, articles and events, subscribe to his newsletter at www.andrewgmarshall.com.

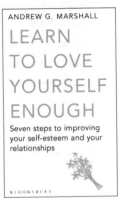

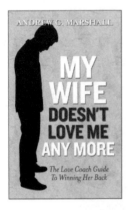